"*Adult Children of Emotionally Immature Parents* is written with the wisdom and heart of a seasoned therapist and the mind of a scholar who's spent decades poring over psychological research and theory. In this book, Lindsay C. Gibson seamlessly blends this impressive body of knowledge with the real-life experiences of her clients to create a user-friendly and highly readable book.... This book is not about blame but rather about understanding oneself on a deep level and learning to heal."

—**Esther Lerman Freeman, PsyD**, clinical associate professor at the Oregon Health and Science University School of Medicine

"Children cannot choose their parents. Unfortunately, many individuals grow up suffering the life-shaping adversities of having emotionally immature, neglectful parents. With wisdom and compassion, Lindsay C. Gibson enables readers to recognize and better understand these toxic relationships and to create novel, healthy paths of healing. This book provides a powerful opportunity for self-help and is a wonderful resource for therapists to recommend to clients in need."

—**Thomas F. Cash, PhD**, Professor Emeritus of psychology at Old Dominion University, and author of *The Body Image Workbook*

"Lindsay C. Gibson's insightful book offers the 'emotionally lonely' a step-by-step journey toward self-awareness and healing. Gibson's revealing anecdotes, enlightening exercises, and honest insight lead the reader to a better understanding of how to connect more fully with oneself and others. This is an excellent book for anyone who feels isolated from family members and seeks to enjoy a more emotionally connected life."

—**Peggy Sijswerda,** editor and publisher of *Tidewater Women* (tidewaterwomen.com) and *Tidewater Family* (tidewaterfamily .com), and author of *Still Life with Sierra*

T0001024

"Lindsay C. Gibson's *Adult Children of Emotionally Immature Parents* is an insightful and compassionate guide for anyone seeking to understand and overcome the long-term impact of growing up in an emotionally barren family. Here you will find sage advice and simple practices that will help you break free from old patterns, connect more deeply with yourself and others, and, ultimately, be the person you were always meant to be."

—**Ronald J. Frederick, PhD**, psychologist and author of
Living Like You Mean It

"Lindsay C. Gibson, a very experienced psychotherapist, wrote *Adult Children of Emotionally Immature Parents* to provide guidance to adults for self-help in resolving anxiety, depression, and relationship difficulties that result from having emotionally immature parents. It is a thorough and detailed description of immature parents, children's experience of their parenting, and methods to resolve the resulting problems. There are many useful examples from Gibson's psychotherapy clients. The book includes helpful exercises for self-understanding. A person can use the book to develop emotional maturity and deeper relationships."

—**Neill Watson, PhD**, research professor and Professor
Emeritus of psychology at the College of William and
Mary, and clinical psychologist who does research on
anxiety, depression, and psychotherapy

"Based on years of reading, research, and working with patients, psychologist Lindsay C. Gibson has written an outstanding book about the multiple ways that emotionally immature parents impact the lives of their adult children. I highly recommend *Adult Children of Emotionally Immature Parents* for all readers who want to understand the parent/child dynamic. This is an uplifting book that provides hope and superb coping strategies for those who find it difficult or impossible to bond with parents who lack empathy and sensitivity.... *Adult Children of Emotionally Immature Parents* is full of wisdom that will enable you to relate to your family members and friends in the healthiest way possible—no matter what age you are—and possibly even to recognize what's behind some of the dysfunctional exchanges depicted in the news and in popular culture."

—**Robin Cutler, PhD**, historian and author of *A Soul on Trial*

"Lindsay C. Gibson's book, *Adult Children of Emotionally Immature Parents*, is filled with clinical vignettes that will resonate with adult children of emotionally immature parents. The book also offers practical advice and exercises for identifying one's true self and avoiding the pitfalls of self-images, relationships, and fantasies that undermine one's psychological well-being. Finally, the book provides solid guidelines for interacting with one's emotionally immature parents in a manner that avoids painful and damaging recreations of the past. Readers will find relief from recognizing that they are not alone and that they are understood by this remarkable clinician."

—**B. A. Winstead, PhD**, professor of psychology at Old
    Dominion University and the Virginia Consortium Program
    in Clinical Psychology, and coeditor of *Psychopathology:
    Foundations for a Contemporary Understanding, Third Edition*

Adult Children *of* Emotionally Immature Parents

How to Heal from Distant, Rejecting, or Self-Involved Parents

LINDSAY C. GIBSON, PsyD

New Harbinger Publications, Inc.

Publisher's Note

This publication is designed to provide accurate and authoritative information in regard to the subject matter covered. It is sold with the understanding that the publisher is not engaged in rendering psychological, financial, legal, or other professional services. If expert assistance or counseling is needed, the services of a competent professional should be sought.

NEW HARBINGER PUBLICATIONS is a registered trademark of New Harbinger Publications, Inc.

New Harbinger Publications is an employee-owned company

Distributed in Canada by Raincoast Books

Copyright © 2015 by Lindsay C. Gibson
New Harbinger Publications, Inc.
5674 Shattuck Avenue
Oakland, CA 94609
www.newharbinger.com

FSC
www.fsc.org
MIX
Paper | Supporting
responsible forestry
FSC® C008955

Cover design by Amy Shoup
Acquired by Tesilya Hanauer
Edited by Jasmine Star

Library of Congress Cataloging-in-Publication Data

Gibson, Lindsay C.
  Adult children of emotionally immature parents : how to heal if your parents couldn't meet your emotional needs / Lindsay C. Gibson.
    pages cm
  Includes bibliographical references.
  ISBN 978-1-62625-170-0 (pbk. : alk. paper) -- ISBN 978-1-62625-171-7 (pdf e-book) -- ISBN 978-1-62625-172-4 (epub) 1. Adult children of dysfunctional families--Mental health. 2. Emotional maturity. 3. Dysfunctional families--Psychological aspects. I. Title.
  RC455.4.F3G53 2015
  616.89'156--dc23   2015005419

Printed in the United States

To Skip, with all my love

Contents

Acknowledgments

Writing this book has been both a personal and professional dream come true. These ideas have been informing my psychotherapy work with clients for a long time, and I've been eager to share them. What I didn't anticipate was how many caring and supportive people would help make this dream become a reality. Receiving this unstinting support fulfilled me in a way that went far beyond just writing the book.

This book began in Hawaii, during a serendipitous meeting with my future acquisitions editor at New Harbinger Publications, Tesilya Hanauer. Tesilya's enthusiasm for the book idea carried me through the long process of development, writing, and editing, and she was always responsive with helpful feedback. She was a tireless champion for the book long before its publication was a sure thing. I am deeply grateful for her faith in me and her unwavering excitement about the idea.

The team at New Harbinger has been more supportive than I could have imagined. Thanks especially to Jess Beebe for her phenomenal editing of the manuscript, especially how she managed to point me in the right direction in a way that made me excited about the changes she proposed. I also extend deep appreciation to Michele Waters, Georgina Edwards, Karen Hathaway, Adia Colar, Katie Parr, and the marketing team at New Harbinger for their extraordinary efforts to make sure this book finds the people who might benefit from it. Many thanks also to Jasmine Star, my excellent copy editor, who tirelessly polished the finished product, creating clarity and flow in a uniquely easy style that enhanced every sentence.

A special thanks to my literary agent, Susan Crawford, who guided me through the minutiae of book publishing—and didn't even mind being called on a camping trip when I had questions. I couldn't have wished for a more helpful agent. Thanks also to Tom Bird, whose writing workshops were invaluable for learning how to write for publication.

I've been lucky to have wonderfully supportive family and friends who cheered me on and, in some cases, were even willing to discuss their own childhood experiences to enrich the book's content. My thanks to Arlene Ingram, Mary Ann Kearley, Judy and Gil Snider, Barbara and Danny Forbes, Myra and Scott Davis, Scotty and Judi Carter, and my cousin and fellow author, Robin Cutler. Also, a special thanks to Lynn Zoll, who kept me going with her "Write on!" e-mails and cards, and to Alexandra Kedrock, whose wisdom elucidated many of the points I struggled to make clear in the book.

Esther Lerman Freeman was truly a friend in need, coming to the rescue numerous times to discuss aspects of the book, and to read and edit on request. Her feedback was invaluable, and her friendship has been essential ever since we began as fellow doctoral students many years ago.

To my wonderful sister, Mary Babcock, my love and deepest thanks for all her devoted support and interest. She has been a mainstay in my life, and her optimism regarding my creative endeavors has kept me inspired. Not many people are as lucky as I am to have the closest of friends, a peerless mentor, and a loyal relative all in one person, but Mary has been all of that.

My son, Carter Gibson, has given me his infectious enthusiasm and "Yay, Mom!" spirit all along the way. I am so thankful to have his exuberance and good sense in my life, and grateful for the way he makes anything seem possible.

And finally, my deepest love and appreciation to my incredible life partner and husband, Skip. All he had to hear was that this book was my life dream, and he stepped forward in every way imaginable to make it come true. In addition to supporting me by taking care of me during the long process of writing, he has been unfailingly invested in the book's mission and my career as a writer. It has been one of the great experiences of my life to be listened to and loved by such a genuine and caring person. In his presence, my true self has flourished.

Introduction

Although we're accustomed to thinking of grown-ups as more mature than their children, what if some sensitive children come into the world and within a few years are more emotionally mature than their parents, who have been around for decades? What happens when these immature parents lack the emotional responsiveness necessary to meet their children's emotional needs? The result is emotional neglect, a phenomenon as real as any physical deprivation.

Emotional neglect in childhood leads to a painful emotional loneliness that can have a long-term negative impact on a person's choices regarding relationships and intimate partners. This book describes how emotionally immature parents negatively affect their children, especially children who are emotionally sensitive, and shows you how to heal yourself from the pain and confusion that come from having a parent who refuses emotional intimacy.

Emotionally immature parents fear genuine emotion and pull back from emotional closeness. They use coping mechanisms that resist reality rather than dealing with it. They don't welcome self-reflection, so they rarely accept blame or apologize. Their immaturity makes them inconsistent and emotionally unreliable, and they're blind to their children's needs once their own agenda comes into play. In this book, you'll learn that when parents are emotionally immature, their children's emotional needs will almost always lose out to the parents' own survival instincts.

Myths and fairy tales have been depicting such parents for centuries. Think of how many fairy tales feature abandoned children who must find aid from animals and other helpers because their parents are careless, clueless, or absent. In some stories, the parent character is actually malevolent and the children must take their survival into their own hands. These stories have been popular for centuries because they touch a common chord: how children must fend for themselves after their parents have neglected or abandoned them. Apparently, immature parents have been a problem since antiquity.

And this theme of emotional neglect by self-preoccupied parents can still be found in the most compelling stories of our popular culture. In books, movies, and television, the story of emotionally immature parents and the effects they have on their children's lives makes for a rich subject. In some stories, this parent-child dynamic is the main focus; in others, it might be depicted in the backstory of a character. As you learn more about emotional immaturity in this book, you may be reminded of famous characters in drama and literature, not to mention the daily news.

Knowing about differences in emotional maturity gives you a way of understanding why you can feel so emotionally lonely in spite of other people's claims of love and kinship. I hope that what you read here will answer questions you've had for a long time, such as why your interactions with some family members have been so hurtful and frustrating. The good news is that by grasping the concept of emotional immaturity, you can develop more realistic expectations of other people, accepting the level of relationship possible with them instead of feeling hurt by their lack of response.

Among psychotherapists, it's long been known that emotionally disengaging from toxic parents is the way to restore peace and self-sufficiency. But how does one do this? We do it by understanding what we are dealing with. What has been missing from the literature on self-involved parents is a full explanation of why there are limits on their ability to love. This book fills that gap, explaining that these parents basically lack emotional maturity. Once you understand their traits, you'll be able to judge for yourself what level of relationship might be possible, or impossible, with your parent. Knowing this allows us to return to ourselves, living life from our own deeper nature instead of focusing on parents who refuse to change. Understanding their emotional immaturity frees us from emotional loneliness as we realize their neglect wasn't about us, but about them. When we see why they can't be different, we can finally be free of our frustration with them, as well as our doubts about our own lovability.

In this book, you'll find out why one or both of your parents couldn't give you the kind of interactions that could have nourished you emotionally. You'll learn exactly why you may have felt so unseen and unknown by your parent, and why your well-meaning efforts at communication never made things better.

In chapter 1, you'll see why people who grew up with emotionally immature parents often feel emotional loneliness. You'll read the stories of people whose lack of deep emotional connections with their parents affected their adult lives in significant ways. You'll get a detailed picture of what emotional loneliness looks like and also see how self-awareness can help reverse feelings of isolation.

Chapters 2 and 3 explore the characteristics of emotionally immature parents and the types of relationship problems they cause. Many of your parent's puzzling behaviors will start to make sense when you see them in the light of emotional immaturity. A checklist is provided to help you identify your parent's areas of emotional immaturity. You'll also gain some insight into possible reasons why your parent's emotional development stopped early.

Chapter 4 describes four main types of emotionally immature parents and will assist you in identifying which type of parenting you may have had. You'll also learn about the self-defeating habits that children can develop in an effort to adapt to these four parent types.

In chapter 5, you'll see how people lose touch with their true selves in order to take on a family role, and how they build up subconscious fantasies about how other people should act in order to heal them from past neglect. You'll learn about the two very different types of children likely to emerge from emotionally immature parenting: internalizers and externalizers. (This will also shed light on why siblings from the same family can be so vastly different in their style of functioning.)

In chapter 6, I describe the internalizer personality in greater detail. This is the personality type most likely to engage in self-reflection and personal growth, and therefore most likely to be drawn to this book.

Internalizers are highly perceptive and sensitive, with strong instincts to engage and connect with other people. You'll see whether this personality type fits you, especially the traits of tending to feel apologetic for needing help, doing most of the emotional work in relationships, and thinking about what other people want first.

Chapter 7 addresses what happens when old patterns of relating finally break down and people begin to wake up to their unmet needs. This is the point at which people are likely to seek help in psychotherapy. I'll share stories of people who woke up from their self-denying patterns and decided to be different. In this process of admitting the truth to themselves, they regained their ability to trust their instincts and truly know themselves.

In chapter 8, I'll introduce a way of relating to people that I call the maturity awareness approach. By using the concept of emotional maturation to assess people's level of functioning, you'll begin to see their behavior in a more objective way and can observe the defining signs of immaturity as they occur. You'll learn what works and doesn't work with emotionally immature people and how to protect yourself from the emotional distress they can cause. All of this will help you gain new peace and self-confidence.

In chapter 9, you'll hear about individuals who have experienced a new sense of freedom and wholeness after using this approach. Their stories will help you see how it feels to finally get free of the guilt and confusion that parental immaturity causes. By focusing on your own self-development, you can get on the road to freedom from emotionally immature relationships.

Chapter 10 describes how to identify people who will treat you well and be emotionally safe and reliable. It will also help you change the self-defeating interpersonal behaviors common to adult children of emotionally immature parents. With this new approach to relationships, emotional loneliness can be a thing of the past.

After reading this book, you'll be able to spot signs of emotional immaturity and understand why you've often felt alone. It will finally make sense why your attempts at emotional intimacy have failed to create closer relationships with emotionally immature people. You'll learn to manage the overdeveloped empathy that may have held you emotionally hostage to manipulative, nonreciprocal people. Finally, you'll be able to recognize people who are capable of genuine emotional intimacy and satisfying communication.

I'm excited to share my results from years of reading and research on this topic, along with fascinating stories drawn from my work with real clients. I've been on a quest to understand this topic for most of my professional life. It seems to me that a great truth has been hiding in plain sight, obscured by the social stereotypes that put parents beyond the reach of objectivity. I'm so happy to share the discoveries and conclusions that have been confirmed over and over again by the many people I've worked with.

My hope is to provide relief from the confusion and emotional suffering that emotionally immature parents arouse in their children. If this book helps you understand your emotional loneliness or helps you create deeper emotional connections and more rewarding intimacy in your life, then I will have accomplished my mission. If it helps you see yourself as a worthy person who is no longer at the mercy of other people's manipulations, I will have done my job. I know you've suspected much of what you are about to read, and I'm here to tell you that you were right all along.

I wish the very best for you.

Chapter 1

How Emotionally Immature Parents Affect Their Adult Children's Lives

E motional loneliness comes from not having enough emotional intimacy with other people. It can start in childhood, due to feeling emotionally unseen by self-preoccupied parents, or it can arise in adulthood when an emotional connection is lost. If it's been a lifelong feeling, it points to the likelihood of not being sufficiently emotionally responded to as a child.

Growing up in a family with emotionally immature parents is a lonely experience. These parents may look and act perfectly normal, caring for their child's physical health and providing meals and safety. However, if they don't make a solid emotional connection with their child, the child will have a gaping hole where true security might have been.

The loneliness of feeling unseen by others is as fundamental a pain as physical injury, but it doesn't show on the outside. Emotional loneliness is a vague and private experience, not easy to see or describe. You might call it a feeling of emptiness or being alone in the world. Some people have called this feeling existential loneliness, but there's nothing existential about it. If you feel it, it came from your family.

Children have no way of identifying a lack of emotional intimacy in their relationship with a parent. It isn't a concept they have. And it's even less likely that they can understand that their parents are emotionally immature. All they have is a gut feeling of emptiness, which is how a child experiences loneliness. With a mature parent, the child's remedy for loneliness is simply to go to the parent for affectionate connection. But if your parent was scared of deep feelings, you might have been left with an uneasy sense of shame for needing comforting.

When the children of emotionally immature parents grow up, the core emptiness remains, even if they have a superficially normal adult life. Their loneliness can continue into adulthood if they unwittingly choose relationships that can't give them enough emotional connection. They may go to school, work, marry, and raise children, but all the while they'll still be haunted by that core sense of emotional isolation. In this chapter, we'll look at people's experience of emotional loneliness, along with how self-awareness helped them understand what they were missing and how to change.

Emotional Intimacy

Emotional intimacy involves knowing that you have someone you can tell anything to, someone to go to with all your feelings, about anything and everything. You feel completely safe opening up to the other person, whether in the form of words, through an exchange of looks, or by just being together quietly in a state of connection. Emotional intimacy is profoundly fulfilling, creating a sense of being seen for who you really are. It can only exist when the other person seeks to know you, not judge you.

As children, the basis for our security is emotional connection with our caretakers. Emotionally engaged parents make children feel that they always have someone to go to. This kind of security requires genuine emotional interactions with parents. Parents who are emotionally mature engage in this level of emotional connection almost all the time. They've developed enough self-awareness to be comfortable with their own feelings, as well as those of other people.

More importantly, they're emotionally attuned to their children, noticing their children's moods and welcoming their feelings with interest. A child feels safe connecting with such a parent, whether seeking comfort or sharing enthusiasm. Mature parents make their children feel that they enjoy engaging with them and that it's fine to talk about emotional issues. These parents have a lively, balanced emotional life and are usually consistent in their attentiveness and interest toward their children. They are emotionally dependable.

Emotional Loneliness

Parents who are emotionally immature, on the other hand, are so self-preoccupied that they don't notice their children's inner experiences. In addition, they discount feelings, and they fear emotional intimacy. They're uncomfortable with their own emotional needs and therefore have no idea how to offer support at an emotional level. Such parents may even become nervous and angry if their children get upset, punishing them instead of comforting them. These reactions shut down children's instinctive urge to reach out, closing the door to emotional contact.

If one or both of your parents weren't mature enough to give you emotional support, as a child you would have felt the effects of not having it, but you wouldn't necessarily have known what was wrong. You might have thought that feeling empty and alone was your own private, strange experience, something that made you different from other people. As a child, you had no way of knowing that this hollow feeling is a normal, universal response to lacking adequate human companionship. "Emotional loneliness" is a term that suggests its own cure: being on the receiving end of another person's sympathetic interest in what you're feeling. This type of loneliness isn't an odd or senseless feeling; it's the predictable result of growing up without sufficient empathy from others.

To round out this description of emotional loneliness, let's look at two people who vividly remember this feeling from childhood and describe it well.

————David's Story————

Here's how my client David responded when I commented that growing up in his family sounded lonely: "It was incredibly lonely, like I was utterly isolated. It was a fact of my existence. It just felt normal. In my family, everyone was separate from each other, and we were all emotionally isolated. We lived parallel lives, with no points of contact. In high school, I used to get this image of floating in the ocean with no one around me. That's how it felt at home."

When I asked him more about the feeling of loneliness, he said, "It was a sensation of emptiness and nothingness. I had no way of knowing that most people didn't feel that way. That feeling was just daily life for me."

──Rhonda's Story──

Rhonda remembered a similar aloneness when she was seven years old, standing by the moving truck outside her family's old house with her parents and three older siblings. Although she was technically with her family, no one was touching her and she felt totally alone: "I was standing there with my family, but nobody had really explained what this move would mean. I felt totally alone, trying to figure out what was going on. I was with my family, but I didn't feel like I was with them. I remember feeling exhausted, wondering how was I going to deal with this on my own. I didn't feel like I could ask any questions. They were totally unavailable to me. I was too anxious to share anything with them. I knew it was on me to cope with this alone."

The Message Within Emotional Loneliness

This kind of emotional pain and loneliness is actually a healthy message. The anxiety felt by David and Rhonda was letting them know that they were in dire need of emotional contact. But because their parents didn't notice how they felt, all they could do was keep their feelings inside. Fortunately, once you start listening to your emotions instead of shutting them down, they will guide you toward an authentic connection with others. Knowing the cause of your emotional loneliness is the first step toward finding more fulfilling relationships.

How Children Cope with Emotional Loneliness

Emotional loneliness is so distressing that a child who experiences it will do whatever is necessary to make some kind of connection with the parent. These children may learn to put other people's needs first as the price of admission to a relationship. Instead of expecting others to provide support or show interest in them, they may take on the role of helping others, convincing everyone that they have few emotional needs of their own. Unfortunately, this tends to create even more loneliness, since covering up your deepest needs prevents genuine connection with others.

Lacking adequate parental support or connection, many emotionally deprived children are eager to leave childhood behind. They perceive that the best solution is to grow up quickly and become self-sufficient. These children become competent beyond their years but lonely at their core. They often jump into adulthood prematurely, getting jobs as soon as they can, becoming sexually active, marrying early, or joining the service. It's as though they're saying, *Since I'm already taking care of myself, I might as well go ahead and get the benefits of growing up fast.* They look forward to adulthood, believing it offers freedom and a chance to belong. Sadly, in their rush to leave home they may end up marrying the wrong person, tolerating exploitation, or staying with a job that takes more than it gives. They often settle for emotional loneliness in their relationships because it feels normal to them, like their early home life.

Why the Past Repeats Itself

If the lack of emotional connection with emotionally immature parents is so painful, why do so many people end up in similarly frustrating relationships in adulthood? The most primitive parts of our brain tell us that safety lies in familiarity (Bowlby 1979). We gravitate to situations we have had experience with because we know how to deal with them. As children, we don't recognize our parents' limitations, because seeing our parents as immature or flawed is frightening. Unfortunately, by denying the painful truth about our parents, we aren't able to recognize similarly hurtful people in future relationships. Denial makes us repeat the same situation over and over because we never see it coming the next time. Sophie's story illustrates this dynamic well.

————Sophie's Story————

Sophie had been dating Jerry for five years. She had a great job as a nurse and felt lucky to have a long-term relationship. At thirty-two, she wanted to get married, but Jerry was in no hurry. In his mind, everything was fine the way it was. He was a fun guy, but he didn't seem to want emotional intimacy and usually closed down when Sophie brought up emotional topics. Sophie was feeling deeply frustrated and sought therapy for help in figuring out what to do. It was a difficult dilemma: she loved Jerry, but she was running out of time to start a family. She also felt guilty and worried that she was asking for too much.

One day Jerry suggested that they go to the restaurant they had gone to on their first date. There was something about the way he asked that made Sophie wonder if he might propose. Sophie barely made it through dinner trying to contain her excitement.

Sure enough, after dinner Jerry pulled a small jewelry box out of his jacket pocket. As he pushed it across the linen tablecloth, Sophie could hardly breathe. But when she opened the box, there was no ring, only a small square of paper with a question mark on it. She didn't understand.

Jerry grinned at her. "Now you can tell your friends I finally popped 'the question'!"

"Are you proposing?" she asked in confusion.

"No, it's a joke. Get it?"

Sophie was shocked, furious, and deeply hurt. When she called her mother and told her about the incident, her mother actually sided with Jerry, telling Sophie it was a funny joke and she shouldn't be mad.

I honestly cannot think of a single situation where this would be a good joke in a relationship. It's too deflating and demeaning. But as Sophie recognized later, her mother and Jerry had a lot in common in their insensitivity to people's feelings. Every time Sophie tried to tell them how she felt, she ended up feeling invalidated.

In therapy, Sophie began to see the parallels between her mother's lack of empathy and Jerry's emotional insensitivity. She realized that in her relationship with Jerry, she had reentered the emotional loneliness she'd felt as a child. She now saw that her frustration with Jerry's emotional unavailability wasn't something new; it was as old as her childhood. Sophie had felt that sense of unconnectedness her whole life.

Feeling Guilty for Being Unhappy

I have a special place in my heart for people like Sophie, who function so well that other people think they have no problems. In fact, their competence makes it hard for them to take their own pain seriously. "I have it all," they're likely to say. "I should be happy. Why do I feel so miserable?" This is the classic confusion of a person whose physical needs were met in childhood while emotional needs remained unfulfilled.

People like Sophie often feel guilty for complaining. Men and women alike will list the things they have to be thankful for, as if their life were an addition problem whose positive sum means nothing can be wrong. But they can't shake the feeling of being fundamentally alone and lacking the level of emotional intimacy they crave in their closest relationships.

By the time they come to see me, some of them are either ready to leave their partner or are involved in an affair that gives them some of what they need. Others have avoided romantic relationships altogether, seeing emotional commitment as a trap they prefer to stay out of. Still others have decided to stay in their relationship for their children and come to therapy for help in learning how to be less angry and resentful.

Few of these people walk into my office with the thought that their lack of satisfying emotional intimacy started in childhood. They are usually mystified as to how they ended up in a life that doesn't make them happy. They struggle with feelings of selfishness for wanting something more out of life. As Sophie initially said, "Relationships are always going to have frustrations. It's work, right?"

She was partly right. Good relationships do take some effort and forbearance. But it shouldn't take work just to be noticed. Making an emotional connection ought to be the easy part.

Emotional Loneliness Transcends Gender

Although women still outnumber men in seeking psychotherapy, I've worked with many men who have faced the same issue of feeling lonely in their primary relationship. In some ways, it's even more poignant for them because our culture maintains that males have fewer emotional needs. But taking a look at the rates of suicide and violence reveals that this isn't true. Men are more likely to become violent or succeed at suicide when they feel emotionally anguished. Men who lack emotional intimacy, a sense of belonging, or caring attention can feel as empty as anybody else, though they may resist showing it. Emotional connection is a basic human need, regardless of gender.

Children who feel they cannot engage their parents emotionally often try to strengthen their connection by playing whatever roles they believe their parents want them to. Although this may win them some fleeting approval, it doesn't yield genuine emotional closeness. Emotionally disconnected parents don't suddenly develop a capacity for empathy just because a child does something to please them.

People who lacked emotional engagement in childhood, men and women alike, often can't believe that someone would want to have a relationship with them just because of who they are. They believe that if they want closeness, they must play a role that always puts the other person first.

14

─────Jake's Story─────

Jake had recently married Kayla, a bubbly woman who made him feel genuinely loved. He was happy when he got married, but now he couldn't shake a feeling of being very down in the dumps. "I should be happy," he said, "I'm the luckiest guy in the world, and I'm trying hard to be the person she wants me to be. But I feel like I'm *acting*, forcing myself to be more upbeat than I really am. I hate feeling like I'm faking it."

I asked Jake who he thought he should be with Kayla.

"I should be a person who is super happy, like she is. I need to make her feel loved and keep her happy. That's the way it's supposed to be." He looked at me expectantly for confirmation, but when I just waited, he went on: "When she comes home from work, I try hard to act really happy and excited, but it's more than I'm really feeling. I'm exhausted."

I asked him what he thought would happen if he were to honestly tell Kayla about the strain he felt, and he said, "She would be devastated and furious if I tried to talk to her about it."

I told Jake that I believed sharing his honest feelings might have enraged someone in his past, but it didn't sound like how Kayla would respond. It sounded more like what he had told me about his angry mother, who was quick to blow up if people didn't do what she wanted.

Jake's secure relationship with Kayla was tempting him to relax and be himself, but he was sure that his relationship would suffer if he stopped trying so hard.

When I told Jake that maybe this safe new relationship was giving him a chance to finally be loved for himself, he was uncomfortable with the reference to his emotional needs. He looked embarrassed and said, "When you say it like that, I sound pitiful and needy."

During childhood, Jake had gotten the message from his mother that showing any emotional needs meant he was weak.

Further, if he didn't act how she wanted him to, he felt inadequate and unlovable.

Jake was eventually able to understand his feelings and become more genuine with Kayla, who totally accepted him. But he was astounded by how much anger toward his mother we'd unearthed. "I can't believe how much I hated her," he said. What Jake didn't realize is that hate is a normal and involuntary reaction when somebody tries to control you for no good reason. It signals that the person is extinguishing your emotional life force by getting his or her needs met at your expense.

Feeling Trapped in Taking Care of Parents

It isn't only in romantic relationships that people may feel deep emotional loneliness. I've worked with single people who have similar stories, but their unhappy adult relationships are played out with parents or friends. Typically, their relationships with their parents are so draining that they don't have the emotional energy to pursue romantic relationships, nor do they want to. Their experiences with their parents have taught them that relationships mean feeling abandoned and burdened at the same time. To these people, relationships feel like traps. They already have their hands full with a parent who acts like he or she owns them.

———Louise's Story———

Louise, a single schoolteacher in her late twenties, felt completely dominated by her controlling mother, a gruff ex-policewoman who expected Louise to live with her and take care of her. Her demands were so excessive that Louise started having suicidal thoughts. Louise's therapist told her in no uncertain terms that her life depended on getting away from her mother's control. When Louise told her mother she was leaving, her mother said,

"That's not going to happen. You'd feel awful about yourself. Besides, I can't get along without you." Fortunately, Louise summoned the strength to establish her own, independent life. In the process, she discovered that guilt was a manageable emotion, and a small price to pay for her freedom.

Not Trusting Your Instincts

Emotionally immature parents don't know how to validate their child's feelings and instincts. Without this validation, children learn to give in to what others seem sure about. As adults, they may deny their instincts to the point where they acquiesce to relationships they don't really want. They may then believe it's up to them to make the relationship work. They may rationalize why they have to try so hard in the relationship, as though it were normal to struggle daily to get along with your mate. While effort is needed to maintain communication and connection in a relationship, it shouldn't feel like constant, unrewarding work.

The truth is, if both partners fit each other, understand each other's feelings, and are positive and supportive, relationships are primarily pleasurable, not arduous. It isn't asking too much to generally feel happy when you see your partner or look forward to time together. When people say, "You can't have everything," they're really saying they don't have what they need.

As a human being, you can trust yourself to know when you're emotionally satisfied. You know when you've been given full measure. You aren't a bottomless pit of ceaseless demands. You can trust the inner prompts that tell you when something is missing.

But if you've been trained to discount your feelings, you'll feel guilty for complaining if everything looks okay on the outside. If you have a place to live, a regular paycheck, enough food, and a partner or friends, conventional wisdom says, "How bad can it be?"

Many people can readily enumerate all the reasons why they should be satisfied and be shy about admitting that they aren't. They blame themselves for not having the "right" feelings.

——Meaghan's Story——

Meaghan broke up with her boyfriend twice before getting pregnant in her first year of college. Although her boyfriend wanted to get married, the relationship just didn't feel right to her. However, her parents were crazy about her boyfriend, who came from a wealthy family, and pushed her to marry him, especially with a baby on the way, and Meaghan gave in. Her husband became a successful real estate broker, adding to his appeal for her parents. Years later, with three children finally in college, she was ready to end her marriage, but she felt confused and guilty about wanting to leave.

In our first session, Meaghan said, "I don't know how to express myself." Neither her husband nor her parents could understand why she wasn't satisfied with the way things were, and she couldn't find the words to defend her feelings. For every explanation she stumbled through, they countered with several reasons why she was wrong. They discounted her reasons because her complaints were emotional, like not being listened to, having her feelings and requests disregarded, and not having any fun with her husband. She tried to explain to them that she and her husband weren't compatible socially, sexually, or in their activities.

Meaghan's real problem wasn't that she didn't know how to express herself; it was that her family didn't want to hear her. Her husband and parents weren't trying to understand; they were focused on trying to convince her she was mistaken.

Meaghan felt embarrassed and guilty because her emotional needs were outweighing her vows and commitments. But as I pointed out to her, vows and promises aren't the fuel relationships run on. Relationships are sustained by the pleasure of emotional intimacy, the feeling that someone is interested in taking the time to really listen and understand your experience. If you don't have that, your relationship won't thrive. Mutual emotional responsiveness is the single most essential ingredient of human relationships.

Meaghan feared she was a bad person for wanting to leave her husband. When people can no longer tolerate an emotionally unrewarding relationship, how should we characterize their desire to leave? Are they being selfish, impulsive, or hard-hearted? Are they giving up prematurely, or perhaps being just plain immoral? If they've taken it all this time, why can't they take it a little more? Why rock the boat?

The point might exactly be that they *have* taken it for so long. Perhaps they've literally used up all the energy they had to give, like Meaghan, who had spent years trying to give her husband and parents what they expected. Meaghan had repeatedly tried to explain her feelings and tell them how unhappy she was. She even tried to get through to her husband by leaving him letters to read. But neither he nor her parents listened. Instead, they responded with what they wanted *her* to do—the classic egocentric response of emotionally immature people.

Fortunately, Meaghan finally began to take her own feelings seriously and quit letting her husband and parents deny her emotional needs with arguments that were emotionally irrelevant to her. When Meaghan finally realized what she really wanted from a relationship, she shyly told me, "I want to matter the most to someone. I want someone to want to be with me." Then she looked confused and said, "Is that too much to ask? I really don't know." Since childhood, Meaghan had been trained to think that her natural desire to feel special and loved was selfish. Throughout her marriage, her husband reinforced this by telling her that she wanted too much and her expectations were too high—until she stopped believing that he knew more about her than she did.

Lacking Self-Confidence Due to Parental Rejection

When parents reject or emotionally neglect their children, these children often grow up to expect the same from other people. They lack confidence that others could be interested in them. Instead of asking for what they want, their low self-confidence makes them shy and conflicted about seeking attention. They're convinced they would be bothering others if they tried to make their needs known. Unfortunately, by expecting past rejection to repeat itself, these children end up stifling themselves and promoting more emotional loneliness.

In this situation, people create their own emotional loneliness by hanging back instead of interacting. As a therapist, my job is to help them realize how their parents have damaged their self-confidence while also encouraging them to tolerate the anxiety of trying something new in order to connect more with others. As the next two stories show, people are capable of doing this; it just may not occur to them to reach out because they simply don't have much experience with other people helping them feel better.

Ben's Story

Ben had suffered from anxiety and depression for much of his life. He characterized his mother as a rejecting woman who kept him at arm's length. She was imperious and had made it clear that he held a low place in the family pecking order. As a child, Ben's needs and feelings simply weren't a primary concern, and he was expected to wait until the adults were ready to pay attention to him.

Fortunately, Ben married a kind and affectionate woman, Alexa. But he was baffled as to why she had chosen him. As he put it, "I'm not a very interesting person. I don't know why Alexa likes me. I'm not exactly a nobody, but…" The way Ben's voice trailed off indicated that he saw himself as someone who could easily be overlooked and taken for granted. Ben's childhood experience of his mother's rejection had clearly deflated his self-confidence. Further, it had convinced him that others would find his emotional needs as repugnant as his mother had.

One day in session, Ben talked about how unhappy and overwhelmed he was feeling. When I asked if he'd confided in Alexa about how he was feeling, he said, "No, I can't. She's got her own stuff to deal with. I don't want her to see me as this wuss who can't deal with his own issues." When I said it seemed unlikely Alexa would do that, he agreed: "I know she loves me for just being myself. But I don't feel that way about myself."

When I suggested to Ben that he could try opening up to Alexa, given how supportive she was, he told me he thought he should be more self-reliant, saying, "I should be able to weather this on my own. Isn't it up to me to meet my own emotional needs?"

What a lonely thought. I told Ben that we all need other people to meet our emotional needs for comfort and closeness. That's what relationships are all about.

————Charlotte's Story————

Charlotte provides another example of this tendency to see current situations through the lens of past parental rejection. She had finally accepted a friend's repeated invitations to enter a short story in a writing contest. She was sure the judges would reject her work, even though she was a successful newspaper journalist. To her astonishment, she won.

For Charlotte, this stirred up painful memories of all the times in childhood when she was criticized and shamed by her parents for trying to stand out. Her parents weren't capable of emotional support and instead found reasons to disparage her accomplishments. Now, even as she was thrilled about her award, she simultaneously felt terrified that someone would step forward to mock her or expose her as undeserving. Instead of sharing her happiness with everyone, she kept it to herself, telling herself no one was interested.

Childhood Loneliness Beneath Adult Success

Parental rejection doesn't always result in low self-confidence. Some intelligent, resilient people somehow manifest the confidence to pursue good careers and reach high levels of achievement. Many find emotionally mature partners, enjoy satisfying long-term relationships, and create close families of their own. But despite their emotional needs being met in current relationships, the lingering trauma of childhood loneliness may haunt them in other ways, through anxiety, depression, or bad dreams.

——Natalie's Story——

Natalie, fifty, an award-winning business consultant, was an emotionally neglected child who nevertheless created a rewarding adult life for herself both personally and professionally. Unfortunately, the emotional neglect she experienced as a child still haunts her in the form of dreams, which she described like this: "I have recurring nightmares with the same theme. I'm in a desperate situation that I can't get out of. I'm trying frantically to find a solution, a way out. Different roads, different keys, different doors—none of them are a solution. I'm all alone, and there's only me trying to solve the problem; there's no one else. Lots of times I'm responsible for other people who are watching and waiting for me to fix everything, but here they give me no help. There is no comfort to be found. I have no protection and I'm not safe. Then I wake up and my heart is racing."

Natalie's dream captures what it feels like to be emotionally alone. She has to deal with everything by herself and doesn't consider asking anyone for help. This is how children of emotionally immature parents feel. Their parents may technically be present, but they offer little help, protection, or comfort.

In her family life, Natalie still takes care of her elderly mother, who lives with Natalie and her husband and kids. But no matter how much Natalie does, her mother still complains that Natalie has never loved her or helped her enough. Since childhood, Natalie has felt the responsibility for her mother's emotional state. Meanwhile, Natalie was on her own because her mother wasn't a person she could turn to. Children like Natalie often grow up as little adults, helping their parents, giving them no trouble, and appearing to need practically nothing. These capable kids may seem like they can parent themselves, but they can't. No child can. They just learn to cling to whatever emotional scraps they get because any connection is better than none at all.

Yet who would guess Natalie's early insecurities as she strides into meetings, all business in her impeccable suits? She has a good marriage, successful children, and close friendships. She knows how to relate to people from all walks of life, and her emotional intelligence is off the charts. Natalie's dreams pull back the curtain to reveal the emotional loneliness that remains within her. Despite creating a fulfilling adult life, inside she remains vulnerable to anxieties about being alone and unsupported. Not until she was nearly fifty did she begin to understand how her relationship with her mother fueled her underlying feelings of anxiety. That was one of the most meaningful discoveries of her life. Finally, she saw the reason for those nightmares.

Why It Feels So Bad to Live Without Emotional Connection

There's a reason why people have such a strong need for emotional connection with others. Throughout human evolution, being part of a group has always meant more safety and less stress. Our ancestors who most disliked separation were more likely to survive because they enjoyed the safe feeling of being close to others. Early humans who didn't mind isolation, on the other hand, may have been comfortable with more distance than was good for their survival.

So when you're longing for a deep emotional connection, remind yourself that your painful feeling of aloneness is coming not just from your individual history, but also from human genetic memory. Just like you, our distant ancestors had a strong need for emotional closeness. Your need for attention and connection is as old as the human race. You have prehistoric reasons for not liking to be lonely.

Summary

A lack of emotional intimacy creates emotional loneliness in both children and adults. Attentive and reliable emotional relationships are the basis of a child's sense of security. Unfortunately, emotionally immature parents are usually too uncomfortable with closeness to give their children the deep emotional connection they need. Parental neglect and rejection in childhood can adversely affect self-confidence and relationships in adulthood, as people repeat old, frustrating patterns and then blame themselves for not being happy. Even adult success doesn't completely erase the effects of parental disconnection earlier in life.

Understanding how your parent's emotional immaturity has affected you is the best way to avoid repeating the past in your adult relationships. To that end, in the next chapter we'll look at the hallmark characteristics of emotionally immature parents.

Chapter 2

Recognizing the Emotionally Immature Parent

I t can be hard to look at your parents objectively because it might feel like you're betraying them. But that isn't the motive here. In this book, our mission is not to disrespect or betray your parents, but to finally see them objectively. I hope you'll see that the discussions of emotionally immature parents in this book are informed by a deep understanding of the reasons for their limitations. As you'll see, much of their immature, hurtful behavior is unintentional. By viewing these and other aspects of your parents more dispassionately, you can understand things about yourself and your history that you might not have thought about before.

Most signs of emotional immaturity are beyond a person's conscious control, and most emotionally immature parents have no awareness of how they've affected their children. We aren't trying to blame these parents, but to understand why they are the way they are. My hope is that any new insights about your parent you gain from reading this book will have the result of radically increasing your own self-awareness and emotional freedom.

Fortunately, as adults, we have the ability and independence to assess whether our parents can really give us the care and understanding we desire. To judge this objectively, it's important to understand not just your parents' superficial behavioral characteristics, but also their underlying emotional framework. Once you understand these deeper traits and learn what to expect from your parents and how to label their behaviors, you're far less likely to be caught unaware by their limitations.

Keep in mind that your thoughts about your parents are private. They may never know what you've gotten from this book, nor do they need to. The goal is for you to gain the self-confidence that comes from knowing the truth of your own story. You aren't betraying your parents by seeing them accurately. Thinking about them objectively can't hurt them. But it can help you.

As you saw in the previous chapter, emotionally immature parents can have devastating impacts on their children's self-esteem and relationships in adulthood. The effects can range from mild to severe, depending on the parent's level of immaturity, but the net effect is the same: the children feel emotionally unseen and lonely. This erodes their children's sense of their own lovability and can lead to excessive caution about emotional intimacy with others.

Exercise: Assessing Your Parent's Emotional Immaturity

Human emotional immaturity has been studied for a long time. However, over the years it has lost ground to an increasing focus on symptoms and clinical diagnosis, using a medical disease model to quantify behaviors as illnesses suitable for insurance reimbursement. But in terms of a deep understanding of people, assessing emotional immaturity is often far more useful, as you're likely to discover when reading this chapter, and by completing this exercise.

Read through the following statements and check any that describe your parent. If you'd like to fill out this assessment for more than one parent or stepparent, use the downloadable version of this exercise available at http://www.newharbinger.com/31700. (See the back of the book for instructions on how to access it.)

_____ My parent often overreacted to relatively minor things.

_____ My parent didn't express much empathy or emotional awareness.

_____ When it came to emotional closeness and feelings, my parent seemed uncomfortable and didn't go there.

_____ My parent was often irritated by individual differences or different points of view.

_____ When I was growing up, my parent used me as a confidant but wasn't a confidant for me.

_____ My parent often said and did things without thinking about people's feelings.

_____ I didn't get much attention or sympathy from my parent, except maybe when I was really sick.

_____ My parent was inconsistent—sometimes wise, sometimes unreasonable.

_____ If I became upset, my parent either said something superficial and unhelpful or got angry and sarcastic.

_____ Conversations mostly centered on my parent's interests.

_____ Even polite disagreement could make my parent very defensive.

_____ It was deflating to tell my parent about my successes because it didn't seem to matter.

_____ Facts and logic were no match for my parent's opinions.

_____ My parent wasn't self-reflective and rarely looked at his or her role in a problem.

_____ My parent tended to be a black-and-white thinker, and unreceptive to new ideas.

How many of these statements describe your parent? Since all these items are potential signs of emotional immaturity, checking more than one suggests you very well may have been dealing with an emotionally immature parent.

Personality Pattern vs. Temporary Emotional Regression

There's a difference between a pattern of emotional immaturity and a temporary emotional regression. Anyone can briefly lose emotional control or become impulsive when tired or stressed. And most of us have plenty to cringe about when we look back on certain moments in our lives.

However, when a person has a personality pattern of emotional immaturity, certain behaviors show up repeatedly. These behaviors are so automatic and unconscious that people are unaware of doing them. Emotionally immature people don't step back and think about how their behavior impacts others. There's no cringe factor for them, so they seldom apologize or experience regret.

Defining Maturity

Before we explore emotional immaturity, let's take a look at emotionally mature functioning. Emotional maturity isn't a murky matter of opinion; it has been well and famously studied.

"Emotional maturity" means a person is capable of thinking objectively and conceptually while sustaining deep emotional connections to others. People who are emotionally mature can function independently while also having deep emotional attachments, smoothly incorporating both into their daily life. They are direct about pursuing what they want, yet do so without exploiting other people. They've differentiated from their original family relationships sufficiently to build a life of their own (Bowen 1978). They have a well-developed sense of self (Kohut 1985) and identity (Erikson 1963) and treasure their closest relationships.

Emotionally mature people are comfortable and honest about their own feelings and get along well with other people, thanks to their well-developed empathy, impulse control, and emotional intelligence (Goleman 1995). They're interested in other people's inner lives and enjoy opening up and sharing with others in an emotionally intimate way. When there's a problem, they deal with others directly to smooth out differences (Bowen 1978).

Emotionally mature people cope with stress in a realistic, forward-looking way, while consciously processing their thoughts and feelings. They can control their emotions when necessary, anticipate the future, adapt to reality, and use empathy and humor to ease difficult situations and strengthen bonds with others (Vaillant 2000). They enjoy being objective and know themselves well enough to admit their weaknesses (Siebert 1996).

Personality Traits Associated with Emotional Immaturity

Emotionally immature people, on the other hand, tend to have quite a different set of behavioral, emotional, and mental characteristics. Because these personality characteristics are all interconnected, people who display one are often prone to the others. In the sections that follow, I'll briefly describe various characteristics of emotionally immature people.

They Are Rigid and Single-Minded

As long as there's a clear path to follow, emotionally immature people can do very well, sometimes reaching high levels of success and prestige. But when it comes to relationships or emotional decisions, their immaturity becomes evident. They are either rigid or impulsive, and try to cope with reality by narrowing it down to something manageable. Once they form an opinion, their minds are closed. There's one right answer, and they can become very defensive and humorless when people have other ideas.

They Have Low Stress Tolerance

Emotionally immature people don't deal with stress well. Their responses are reactive and stereotyped. Instead of assessing the situation and anticipating the future, they use coping mechanisms that deny, distort, or replace reality (Vaillant 2000). They have trouble admitting mistakes and instead discount the facts and blame others. Regulating emotions is difficult for them, and they often overreact. Once they get upset, it's hard for them to calm down, and they expect other people to soothe them by doing what they want. They often seek comfort in intoxicants or medication.

They Do What Feels Best

Young children are ruled by feelings, whereas adults consider possible consequences. As we mature, we learn that what feels good isn't always the best thing to do. Among emotionally immature people, however, the childhood instinct to do what feels good never really changes (Bowen 1978). They make decisions on the basis of what feels best in the moment and often follow the path of least resistance.

If you're a mature person and think before you act, you might find it hard to imagine living by what feels good in the moment. So here's an example of the jaw-dropping behavior of the emotionally immature person. Anna convinced her brother, Tom, to come with her to talk to their elderly father about going into assisted living. After visiting with their father a bit, the time came to talk seriously. Suddenly, Tom was nowhere to be found. Anna searched the house and then looked out the front window in time to see her brother getting in his car and leaving. Anna was incredulous and wondered how Tom could run out like that. But when you realize that, in that moment, walking out of the house felt much better than staying for a difficult confrontation, it makes sense.

They Are Subjective, Not Objective

Emotionally immature people assess situations in a subjective way, not objectively. They don't do much dispassionate analysis. When they interpret situations, how they are feeling is more important than what is actually happening. What is true doesn't matter nearly as much as what *feels* true (Bowen 1978). Trying to get a subjectively oriented person to be objective about anything is an exercise in futility. Facts, logic, history—all fall on deaf ears where the emotionally immature are concerned.

They Have Little Respect for Differences

Emotionally immature people are annoyed by other people's differing thoughts and opinions, believing everyone should see things their way. The idea that other people are entitled to their own point of view is beyond them. They may be prone to making social gaffes because they don't have enough awareness of other people's individuality to avoid being offensive. They're only comfortable in role-defined relationships where everyone holds the same beliefs. The quieter, nicer ones are the same, but in a quieter, nicer way.

They Are Egocentric

Normal children are egocentric as youngsters, but the self-involvement of emotionally immature adults is more *childish* than *childlike*. Unlike children, their egocentrism lacks joy and openness. Emotionally immature people are self-preoccupied in an obsessed way, not with the innocence of a child. Young children are self-centered because they're still commanded by pure instinct, but emotionally immature adults are commanded by anxiety and insecurity, like wounded people who must keep checking their intactness. They live in a perpetual state of insecurity, fearing that they'll be exposed as bad, inadequate, or unlovable. They keep their defenses high so other people can't get close enough to threaten their shaky sense of self-worth.

Before you start feeling too sorry for them, keep in mind that their defenses work seamlessly to keep these underlying anxieties below the level of awareness. They would never see themselves as being insecure or defensive.

They Are Self-Preoccupied and Self-Involved

Anxious self-preoccupation is a quality all emotionally immature people share. They're constantly monitoring whether their needs are being met or whether something has offended them. Their self-esteem rises or falls depending on how others react to them. They can't stand to be criticized, so they minimize their mistakes. Because their self-involvement is all-consuming, other people's feelings are eclipsed by their needs. For instance, after one woman told her mother how much it hurt to hear criticisms of her father, her mother said, "Well, if I couldn't tell you, I wouldn't have anybody to talk to."

Terms like "self-absorbed" and "narcissistic" make it sound as if these people enjoy thinking about themselves all the time, but they really have no choice in the matter. They have fundamental doubts about their core worth as human beings. They are profoundly self-involved because their development was stunted by anxiety during childhood. In this way, their egocentrism is more like the self-preoccupation of someone with a chronic pain condition, rather than someone who can't get enough of himself or herself.

They Are Self-Referential, Not Self-Reflective

Emotionally immature people are highly self-referential, meaning that in any interaction, all roads lead back to them. However, they aren't self-reflective. Their focus on themselves isn't about gaining insight or self-understanding; it's about being the center of attention.

As you talk to them, self-referential people will turn whatever you say back to one of their own experiences. An example would be a mother listening to her daughter describe a relationship crisis and using it as a springboard to talk about her own divorce. Another example would be parents who upstage their child's victory with recollections of their own accomplishments.

Those who are more socially skilled might listen more politely, but you still won't hold their interest. They may not overtly change the subject, but they won't ask follow-up questions or express curiosity about the details of your experience. They're more likely to bring the conversation to a close with a pleasant comment that effectively ends it, such as "That's wonderful, dear. I know you had a good time."

Because they lack self-reflection, emotionally immature people don't consider their role in a problem. They don't assess their behavior or question their motives. If they caused a problem, they dismiss it by saying they didn't intend to hurt you. After all, you can't blame them for something they didn't mean to do, right? In this way, their egocentric focus remains on their intention, not the impact on you.

They Like to Be the Center of Attention

Like children, emotionally immature people usually end up being the center of attention. In groups, the most emotionally immature person often dominates the group's time and energy. If other people allow it, all the group's attention will go to that person, and once this happens, it's hard to redirect the group's focus. If anyone else is going to get a chance to be heard, someone will have to force an abrupt transition—something many people aren't willing to do.

You may wonder whether these people are just being extroverted. They aren't. The difference is that most extroverts easily follow a change of topic. Because extroverts crave interaction, not just an audience, they're interested and receptive when others participate. Extroverts do like to talk, but not with the purpose of shutting everyone else down.

They Promote Role Reversal

Role reversal is a hallmark of emotionally immature parenting. In this case, the parent relates to the child as if the child were the parent, expecting attentiveness and comfort from the child. These parents may reverse roles and expect their child to be their confidant, even for adult matters. Parents who discuss their marriage problems with their children are an example of this kind of reversal. Other times parents might expect their children to praise them and be happy for them, just as a child might expect from a parent.

One woman I worked with, Laura, remembered her father running off with another woman, leaving Laura, then just eight years old, to cope with her severely depressed mother on her own. One day Laura's father picked her up in a new convertible, giddy with excitement over his new toy. He expected her to be as thrilled as he was, never considering the contrast between his joyful new life and the gloom Laura lived in with her abandoned mother.

Here's another example of a father who expected his daughter to function in an approving, almost parental role, in spite of his past abuse of her.

Frieda's Story

Frieda, a woman in her late thirties, had grown up in a household dominated by fear. Her father, Martin, tended to express his emotional immaturity through physical aggression. Although he was an upstanding citizen at work and in public life, at home he slapped his children and beat them with a belt to the point of leaving marks. When Frieda finally stood up to him as a teenager he stopped beating her, but he kept it up with her younger sister. He was also verbally demeaning to Frieda's mother.

Martin was an unpredictable man, sometimes impatient and angry, sometimes generous, happy, and loving, depending on how his day was going. But in general, rather than being a parent to his children, Martin expected them to soothe his feelings, make him the center of attention, and exhibit self-control. In a classic case of role reversal, he demanded their unconditional approval while he indulged his own moods like a child. Frieda was especially the target of this role reversal, with Martin clearly expecting her to show an almost maternal love and admiration for him.

For example, after Frieda had moved out to her own townhouse, Martin decided she needed a porch swing—and not just any swing, but one he made himself from heavy lumber. Without asking, he had it delivered to her small deck, where it took up most of the space she had to enjoy sitting outside. It was huge and impossible to move around, which struck Frieda as the perfect analogy for how Martin took up all the space in the family.

He was as proud of himself as a kid who had just presented his mother with an art project. Fortunately, after understanding her father's immaturity and the dynamics involved in their role reversal, Frieda felt free to have the swing removed, restoring her deck to the way she liked it.

They Have Low Empathy and Are Emotionally Insensitive

Impaired empathy is a central characteristic of emotionally immature people, as is avoidance of emotional sharing and intimacy. Being out of touch with their own deeper feelings, they're strikingly blind to how they make other people feel.

Empathy isn't just a social nicety, like being tactful. It's a necessity for true emotional intimacy. You can't have a deep relationship without it. My favorite definition of empathy comes from infant attachment researchers Klaus and Karin Grossman and Anna Schwan, who described empathy as a sensitive mother's ability "to see and to feel states and intentions from the baby's point of view" (1986, 127). This definition includes being aware of both emotions and intentions. Beyond just sympathy, it entails correctly reading people's interests and how their will is being directed.

The highest form of empathy requires an effort of imagination, which has been called mentalization (Fonagy and Target 2008), meaning the ability to imagine that other people have their own unique minds and thought processes. Developmental psychologists refer to this as having a theory of mind. Acquiring this ability is an important developmental milestone for children. Mentalizing allows you to grasp other people's viewpoints and overall inner experience because you realize they have a mind of their own, different from yours. Good parents are excellent at empathizing and mentalizing; their interest in their child's mind makes the child feel seen and understood. It's also an indispensable characteristic for leadership in business, the military, or any situation where understanding and predicting the motives of others is central. Empathy is a bedrock component of emotional intelligence (Goleman 1995), which is essential to social and occupational success.

In his conversations with the Dalai Lama, psychologist Paul Ekman distinguished between different types of empathy and compassion. True empathy involves more than knowing what people feel; it also entails the ability to *resonate* with those feelings (Dalai Lama and Ekman 2008). For example, sociopaths may do an excellent job of reading a person's emotional vulnerabilities, but without the ability to resonate with the other person's feelings, knowledge of those feelings becomes a tool for predation, not connection.

This casts light on a curious fact about emotionally immature people. In spite of not resonating empathically, they are often quite canny when it comes to reading other people's intentions and feelings. However, they don't use their understanding of people to foster emotional intimacy. Instead, their empathy operates at an instinctual or superficially sentimental level. You may feel sized up, but not felt for.

Lack of resonant empathy suggests a lack of self-development. For parents to accurately imagine what their children are feeling, they need to have enough self-development to be aware of their own emotions. If they haven't developed their own emotional self-awareness, they can't resonate with how others, including their own children, might feel inside.

Why There Are So Many Emotionally Immature Parents

Many of my clients have shared stories that reflect the emotional immaturity of their parents. For me, this begs the question of what could have caused so much emotional underdevelopment in so many parents. Based on my observations and clinical experience, it seems likely that the parents of many of my clients were emotionally shut down as children.

As my clients and I have explored their family histories, they've often recalled evidence of great unhappiness and tension in their parents' early lives. Substance abuse, abandonment, loss, abuse, or traumatic immigration experiences hover in the family background, suggesting an atmosphere of loss, pain, and disconnection. Many people have told me that although they felt discounted or abused, it was nothing compared to the stories their parents told about their own childhood misery. Often the relationship between a client's mother and maternal grandmother was conflictual and unsatisfying, even though that grandmother might have become a nurturing figure for the client. It seems that many of my clients' parents never had a supportive or emotionally intimate connection with their own parents, so they developed tough defenses to survive their own emotional loneliness early in life.

It's also important to remember that old-school parenting—the upbringing my clients' parents experienced—was very much about children being seen but not heard. Physical punishment was not only acceptable, it was condoned, even in schools, as the way to make children responsible. For many parents, "spare the rod and spoil the child" was considered conventional wisdom. They weren't concerned about children's feelings; they saw parenting as being about teaching children how to behave. It wasn't until 1946 that Dr. Benjamin Spock, in the original version of his megaseller *The Common Sense Book of Baby and Child Care*, widely popularized the idea that children's feelings and individuality were important factors to consider, in addition to physical care and discipline. In the generations before this shift, parenting tended to focus on obedience as the gold standard of children's development, rather than thinking about supporting children's emotional security and individuality.

In the following stories, you can see the passed-down effects of this old-school parenting on my clients.

————Ellie's Story————

Ellie, the oldest child in a large family, remembered her mother, Trudy, as "a generous person, but hard as a rock." Trudy was active at church and in the community and had a reputation as being kind and helpful. But when it came to empathy for her children's feelings, she was impervious. Ellie had frequent nightmares and depended on a favorite stuffed animal to soothe her. One night, when Ellie was about eleven years old, her mother suddenly took her comforting stuffed animal and said, "I'm giving this away. You're too old for this." When Ellie begged her mother not to, Trudy told her she was being ridiculous. Although Trudy took good care of Ellie physically, she had no feeling for Ellie's emotional attachment to a precious toy.

Ellie was also deeply attached to a cat who had been in the family since she was a toddler. One day, when Ellie came home from school, Trudy announced that she had given the cat away because it had messed in the house. Ellie was devastated, but as Trudy told Ellie years later, "We didn't give a damn about your feelings; we just kept a roof over your heads."

Sarah's Story

Sarah, whose mother was emotionally inhibited and standoffish, had a very strict upbringing. She remembers that her mother always seemed to be holding herself back emotionally, as if behind a great wall. But Sarah cherishes a memory of a morning when her mother stood quietly by her bed, fondly watching Sarah sleep before waking her up. Sarah was already partly awake, but she didn't move so she could enjoy this moment of secret closeness with her mother. Once she was fully awake, the wall went back up and her mother kept a "proper" distance.

Deeper Effects of Being Emotionally Shut Down

Of course, emotionally immature parents were once children themselves, and as children they may have had to shut down many of their deepest feelings in order to be acceptable to their own parents. It's likely that Ellie's and Sarah's mothers also grew up with parental insensitivity toward their feelings. Many emotionally immature people were "overpruned" early in life, growing up within a very limited range of acceptability. Their personalities are like stunted bonsai trees, trained to grow in unnatural shapes. Because they had to bend to fit their families, they were unable to develop fluidly into the integrated, natural people they might have become.

It may be that many emotionally immature people weren't allowed to explore and express their feelings and thoughts enough to develop a strong sense of self and a mature, individual identity. This made it hard for them to know themselves, limiting their ability to engage in emotional intimacy. If you don't have a basic sense of who you are as a person, you can't learn how to emotionally engage with other people at a deep level. This arrested self-development gives rise to additional, deeper personality weaknesses that are common among emotionally immature people, as outlined in this chapter.

They Are Often Inconsistent and Contradictory

Instead of having a well-integrated sense of who they are, emotionally immature people are more like an amalgam of various borrowed parts, many of which don't go together well. Because they had to shut down important parts of themselves out of fear of their parents' reactions, their personalities formed in isolated clumps, like pieces of a puzzle that don't fit together. This explains their inconsistent reactions, which make them so difficult to understand.

Because they probably weren't allowed to express and integrate their emotional experiences in childhood, these people grow up to be emotionally inconsistent adults. Their personalities are weakly structured, and they often express contradictory emotions and behaviors. They step in and out of emotional states, never noticing their inconsistency. When they become parents, these traits create emotional bafflement in their children. One woman described her mother's behavior as chaotic, "flip-flopping in ways that made no sense."

This inconsistency means that, as parents, emotionally immature people may be either loving or detached, depending on their mood. Their children feel fleeting moments of connection with them but don't know when or under what conditions their parent might be emotionally available again. This sets up what behavioral psychologists call an intermittent reward situation, meaning that getting a reward for your efforts is possible but completely unpredictable. This creates a tenacious resolve to keep trying to get the reward, because once in a while these efforts do pay off.

In this way, parental inconsistency can be the quality that binds children most closely to their parent, as they keep hoping to get that infrequent and elusive positive response.

Growing up with an inconsistent parent is likely to undermine a child's sense of security, keeping the child on edge. Since a parent's response provides a child's emotional compass for self-worth, such children also are likely to believe that their parent's changing moods are somehow their fault.

———Elizabeth's Story———

Elizabeth's mother was emotionally unpredictable and kept her guessing. She always felt anxious when approaching her mother. Would her mother push her away, or would she be interested and engaged? Elizabeth told me, "I had to read her moods constantly. If she seemed negative, I would keep my distance. But if she was in a good mood, I could talk to her. She had the power to make me happy, and I tried my best to win her approval." As a child, Elizabeth often worried that she had caused her mother's negative mood changes. Feeling responsible, Elizabeth came to the conclusion I must be flawed.

Elizabeth wasn't a flawed child, but the only way she could make sense of her mother's moods was to think they resulted from something she did—or worse, something she was.

They Develop Strong Defenses That Take the Place of the Self

Instead of learning about themselves and developing a strong, cohesive self in early childhood, emotionally immature people learned that certain feelings were bad and forbidden. They unconsciously developed defenses against experiencing many of their deeper feelings. As a result, energies that could have gone toward developing a full self were instead devoted to suppressing their natural instincts, resulting in a limited capacity for emotional intimacy.

Not realizing the magnitude of their parents' developmental limitations, many children of emotionally immature people think there must be a genuine, fully developed person hiding inside the parent, a real self they could connect to if only their parent would let them. This is especially true if the parent was occasionally affectionate or attentive.

As one woman told me, "With my parents, I used to pick the good part of them I liked and pretend *that* was the real part. I would tell myself that this good part would eventually win out, but it never did take over. I also used to pretend that the hurtful parts of them weren't real. But now I realize it's *all* real."

When people's defenses have become an integral part of their personality, they're as real as scar tissue in the body. It may not have belonged there originally, but once formed, it's enduring. These limitations become a major part of people's personalities. Whether they can ultimately become more authentic and emotionally available depends on their ability to self-reflect.

People often wonder whether their parents can ever change. That depends on whether their parents are willing to self-reflect, which is the first step in any change. Unfortunately, if their parents aren't interested in noticing their impacts on others, they have no impetus to look at themselves; without such self-reflection, there's no way to change.

———Hannah's Story———

Hannah had always longed for a more intimate relationship with her stern, hardworking mother. As an adult, on one visit she asked her mother to tell her something about herself that she'd never shared with Hannah before. This caught her mother off guard. First she looked like a deer in headlights, then she burst into tears and couldn't speak. Hannah felt that she had simultaneously terrified and overwhelmed her mother with this innocent inquiry. She had unwittingly gone straight through her mother's defenses to a long-hidden place of sorrow, exposing her mother's unmet childhood longing to be heard by someone who was interested in her experience. Hannah's interest and empathy overwhelmed the defenses her mother had developed in response to the lack of that kind of connection. She simply couldn't deal with Hannah's attempt at emotional intimacy.

Incomplete Development Leads to Emotional Limitations

Despite being highly emotionally reactive, emotionally immature people have a paradoxical relationship with emotions. They're quick to get emotionally aroused, but they're scared of their most authentic feelings. This is to be expected if they were raised in a family milieu that didn't help them deal with their emotions, or that may even have punished them for being upset. The sooner they can avoid their feelings or get over them, the better. They find the world of deep emotions extremely threatening.

They Fear Feelings

As children, many emotionally immature people grew up in homes where they were taught that the spontaneous expression of certain feelings was a shameful breach of family custom. They learned that expressing, or even experiencing, these deeper feelings could bring shame or punishment, resulting in what psychotherapy researcher Leigh McCullough and her colleagues have called affect phobia (McCullough et al. 2003). Having learned to link their most personal emotions with judgments about being bad, they could no longer stand to acknowledge certain feelings, especially those related to emotional intimacy. As a result, they anxiously sought to inhibit their genuine reactions, developing defensive behaviors instead of experiencing their true feelings and impulses (Ezriel 1952).

Affect phobia can lead to an inflexible, narrow personality based on rigid defenses against certain feelings. As adults, these emotionally immature people have an automatic anxiety reaction when it comes to deep emotional connection. Most genuine emotion makes them feel exposed and extremely nervous. Throughout life, their energy has been devoted to creating a defensive facade that protects them from emotional vulnerability with other people. To avoid dangerous emotional intimacy, they stick to a well-worn life script and resist talking about or processing emotions, including in relationships.

As parents, they pass down this fear of vulnerable emotions to their children. In such families, the saying "I'll give you something to cry about" is a common parental response to an upset child. Many children of emotionally phobic parents develop the fear that if they start crying, they'll never stop, which arises because they were never allowed to find out that crying naturally stops on its own when allowed its full expression. Because they grew up with emotionally phobic parents who stepped in to squelch their distress, they never experienced the natural rhythm of a crying episode and how it winds down.

It's easy to see how children growing up under these conditions could become fearful of their own emotions. In fact, even positive feelings of joy and excitement can become associated with anxiety. For example, Anthony recalled a painful incident when he joyfully raced out the front door to greet his father as he pulled up in the driveway. Anthony leaped over a small bush, swiped it with his foot, and knocked it over. Instead of appreciating Anthony's display of affection, his father gave him a beating. As a result, Anthony learned not only to be afraid of his father, but to fear spontaneous joy as something that would get him in trouble.

They Focus on the Physical Instead of the Emotional

Emotionally immature parents can do a good job of taking care of their children's physical and material needs. In the world of food, shelter, and education, these parents may be able to provide everything that's needed. In terms of things that are physical, tangible, or activity related, many of these parents make sure their children get every advantage they can afford. But when it comes to emotional matters, they can be oblivious to their children's needs.

Many of my clients have good memories of being well cared for when ill, enjoying their parents' attention and even receiving presents and favorite foods. But this happened only after their parents were duly convinced they were really sick. They experienced this attentiveness when they were sick as proof of their parent's love. It seemed to be the one time when they remembered receiving lots of attention.

This makes sense, because caretaking during illness would allow a parent the justification to "indulge" a child with attention and affection. It stands to reason that affectionate caretaking felt safe to these parents when done for the purpose of restoring the child's physical health. Physical aid was more sanctioned than emotional attachment.

Being well cared for in nonemotional areas can create confusion in people who grow up feeling emotionally lonely. They have overwhelming physical evidence that their parents loved and sacrificed for them, but they feel a painful lack of emotional security and closeness with their parents.

They Can Be Killjoys

Fear of genuine emotion can cause emotionally immature people to be killjoys. As parents, instead of enjoying their children's excitement and enthusiasm, they may abruptly change the subject or warn them not to get their hopes up. In response to their children's exuberance, they're likely to say something dismissive or skeptical to bring it down a notch. When one woman told her mother about her excitement about buying her first house, her mother actually said, "Yes, and then you'll find something else to go on about."

They Have Intense but Shallow Emotions

Emotionally immature people are easily overwhelmed by deep emotion, and they display their uneasiness by transmuting it into quick reactivity. Instead of feeling things deeply, they react superficially. They may be emotionally excitable and show a strong sentimentality, perhaps being easily moved to tears. Or they may puff up in anger toward anything they dislike. Their reactivity may seem to indicate that they're passionate and deeply emotional, but their emotional expression often has a glancing quality, almost like a stone skipping the surface rather than going into the depths. It's a fleeting reaction of the moment—dramatic but not deep.

When interacting with such people, the weirdly shallow quality of their emotions may leave you feeling unmoved by their distress. You might tell yourself that you should be feeling more for them, but your heart can't resonate with their exaggerated reactions. And because they overreact so frequently, you may quickly learn to tune them out for the sake of your own emotional survival.

They Don't Experience Mixed Emotions

The ability to feel mixed emotions is a sign of maturity. If people can blend contradictory emotions together, such as happiness with guilt, or anger with love, it shows that they can encompass life's emotional complexity. Experienced together, opposing feelings tame each other. Once people develop the ability to feel different emotions at the same time, the world ripens into something richer and deeper. Instead of having a single, intense, one-dimensional emotional reaction, they can experience several different feelings that reflect the nuances of the situation. However, the reactions of emotionally immature people tend to be black-and-white, with no gray areas. This rules out ambivalence, dilemmas, and other emotionally complicated experiences.

Differences in Quality of Thought

In addition to emotional and behavioral differences, there are often intellectual differences between emotionally mature and immature people. If your parents grew up in a family atmosphere that was full of anxiety and judgment, they may have learned to think narrowly and resist complexity. Excessive childhood anxiety leads not only to emotional immaturity but also to oversimplified thinking that cannot hold opposing ideas in mind. Repressive or punitive family environments typically don't encourage free thinking or self-expression and therefore aren't conducive to fully developing one's mind.

Difficulties with Conceptual Thinking

Starting in adolescence, children begin to think conceptually, enabling them to solve problems with logic and reasoning instead of knee-jerk impulses. Accelerated brain development means they become both more objective and more imaginative. They can group ideas in categories and quickly think in symbols. They go beyond simply memorizing things and start to evaluate ideas, not just compare facts. They are able to think independently and hypothetically, and to generate new insights from previous knowledge. As children enter their teen years, their ability to self-reflect skyrockets because they become able to think about their own thinking (Piaget 1963).

However, the intense emotions and anxiety that emotionally immature people experience can decrease their ability to think at this higher level. Since they are often at the mercy of their emotions, their higher thinking can easily fall apart under stress. In fact, their frequent lack of self-reflection comes from this tendency to regress and temporarily lose their ability to think about their thinking. When emotion-inducing topics come up, their minds fall into rigid black-or-white thinking that rejects complexity and precludes any cross-pollination of ideas.

Emotionally immature people who are otherwise intelligent can think conceptually and show insight as long as they don't feel too threatened in the moment. Their intellectual objectivity is limited to topics that aren't emotionally arousing to them. This can be puzzling to their children, who experience two very different sides to their parents: sometimes intelligent and insightful, other times narrow-minded and impossible to reason with.

Proneness to Literal Thinking

If you listen to the conversations of emotionally immature people, you may notice how routine and literal their thinking is. They tend to talk about what happened or what they observed, not the world of feelings or ideas. For example, one man found his mother's phone conversations draining and boring because she never talked about anything substantive. Instead, she only asked him mundane questions, like what he was doing at the moment or what the weather was like. He told me, "She just reports the facts and never talks about anything other than 'Here's what's happened lately.' She doesn't connect with me in the conversation. I get so frustrated and want to say, 'Can't we talk about something meaningful?' But she can't."

Intellectualizing Obsessively

Another cognitive sign of emotional immaturity is overintellectualizing and getting obsessed about certain topics. In those areas, emotionally immature people can conceptualize well—indeed, excessively. But they don't apply that ability to self-reflection or being emotionally sensitive toward others. Their preoccupation with ideas distracts them from emotional intimacy. They may discuss their favorite topics at length, but they don't really engage the other person. As a result, they can be as hard to talk to as overly literal thinkers. Although they can think conceptually while communicating their ideas, they're only comfortable if things stay on an impersonal and intellectual level.

Summary

Emotional immaturity is a real phenomenon that has been studied and written about for a long time. It undermines people's ability to deal with stress and to be emotionally intimate with others. Emotionally immature people often grew up in a family environment that curtailed their full emotional and intellectual development. As a result, they have an oversimplified approach to life, narrowing situations down to fit their rigid coping skills. Having such a limited sense of self makes them egocentric and undermines their ability to be sensitive to other people's needs and feelings. Their reactive emotions, lack of objectivity, and fear of emotional intimacy can make close relationships difficult, especially when it comes to their children.

In the next chapter, we'll take a look at what it feels like to have a relationship with an emotionally immature parent, along with the challenges adult children face in trying to communicate with such parents.

Chapter 3

How It Feels to Have a Relationship with an Emotionally Immature Parent

In this chapter, I'll explore how emotionally immature parents handle relationships in ways that frustrate their children's emotional needs. As you probably already know, being raised by such a parent feels both lonely and exasperating.

We don't get a vote on our earliest relationships in life. Our strongest bond is to our primary attachment parent, the one we turn to first if scared, hungry, tired, or ill. We may seek out others for play when we're feeling good, but stress or an urgent need will send us scampering back to that principal caretaker (Ainsworth 1967).

The intensity of this early bond helps explain why emotionally immature parents can be so endlessly disappointing. Relationships with them can be hard to deal with, but when we are distant or separated from them, it feels like something essential is missing. Our earliest instincts prompt us to keep turning to our parents for care and understanding.

Exercise: Assessing Your Childhood Difficulties with an Emotionally Immature Parent

Emotional immaturity shows itself most clearly in relationships, and its impacts are especially profound when the relationship is between a parent and child. Read through the following statements, which outline some of the most painful difficulties emotionally immature parents cause for their children, and check off all that reflect your childhood experience. If you'd like to fill out the assessment for more than one parent or stepparent, use the downloadable version of this exercise available at http://www.newhar binger.com/31700. (See the back of the book for instructions on how to access it.)

_____ I didn't feel listened to; I rarely received my parent's full attention.

_____ My parent's moods affected the whole household.

_____ My parent wasn't sensitive to my feelings.

_____ I felt like I should have known what my parent wanted without being told.

_____ I felt like I could never do enough to make my parent happy.

_____ I was trying harder to understand my parent than my parent was trying to understand me.

_____ Open, honest communication with my parent was difficult or impossible.

_____ My parent thought people should play their roles and not deviate from them.

_____ My parent was often intrusive or disrespectful of my privacy.

_____ I always felt that my parent thought I was too sensitive and emotional.

_____ My parent played favorites in terms of who got the most attention.

_____ My parent stopped listening when he or she didn't like what was being said.

_____ I often felt guilty, stupid, bad, or ashamed around my parent.

_____ My parent rarely apologized or tried to improve the situation when there was a problem between us.

_____ I often felt pent-up anger toward my parent that I couldn't express.

Each of these statements is linked to characteristics described in this chapter. Your parent may not have all the characteristics I describe, but checking off more than one of the items suggests some level of emotional immaturity.

Communication Is Difficult or Impossible

If you've been trying to relate to an emotionally immature parent with poor intimacy skills, these interactions may have made you feel shut down, shut up, or shut out. Even if your parent is at the nicer, warmer end of the spectrum, he or she probably has a very narrow window of attention regarding other people's interests. You may have tried for years to find a way to connect, only to come away feeling invisible and unheard time and again. You've probably felt plenty of exasperation; your parent's insensitivity guarantees it.

As one person said about her self-preoccupied mother, "She thinks we are so close, but for me it's not a satisfying relationship. It makes me crazy when she tells people that I'm her best friend."

Communication with emotionally immature people usually feels one-sided. They aren't interested in reciprocal, mutual conversations. Like young children, they crave exclusive attention and want everyone to be interested in what they find engaging. If other people are getting more attention, they find ways to draw attention back to themselves, such as interrupting, firing off zingers that get everybody's attention, or changing the subject. If all else fails, they may pointedly withdraw, look bored, or otherwise communicate that they're disengaged—behaviors that ensure the focus stays on them.

────Brenda's Story────

Brenda's elderly mother, Mildred, had always been very self-centered. After Mildred visited her over the holidays, Brenda was exhausted. At our next session, Brenda looked spent and physically older. During that session, she offered this description of her mother: "My mother is only interested in herself. She never asks me how I'm feeling or how work is going. She only wants to know what I'm doing so she can brag about me to her friends. I don't think she's ever really taken in anything I've said to her; it just doesn't register. We've never had a real relationship because the attention was always on her. She's never filled up my emotional tank. She doesn't care if I'm really happy, and she's very dismissive of whatever I say. Having her around is nothing but work for me. It's like dealing with this superficial person who just wants me to do things for her. I don't know how she has the nerve to be so demanding."

Although Mildred was in her eighties, her egocentrism was childlike. Brenda understood her mother's immaturity at an intellectual level but still found herself getting angry with her. As she told me, "I wish she didn't get under my skin so easily. I'm disappointed at how angry I get when I'm around her." During Mildred's visit, Brenda repeatedly tried to get her settled so she could get a few things done for the holidays. But within minutes Mildred would be calling out to her, expecting Brenda to drop everything and bring her something. It was annoying to be repeatedly interrupted, but Brenda's strong reaction went deeper than that. The following section, on emotional attachment, helps explain Brenda's anger.

They Provoke Anger

John Bowlby, a pioneer in studying children's reactions to separation and loss, observed that babies and children get angry as a normal response to being left by their parents. Sadness is an expected response to loss, but Bowlby documented that anger is also common in response to separation (1979). This is understandable. Anger and even rage are adaptive reactions to feelings of abandonment, giving us energy to protest and change unhealthy emotional situations.

In this light, Brenda's anger at her mother wasn't petty or irrational; it was her biological response to feelings of helplessness caused by her mother's emotional disregard. After all, feeling dismissed or unseen creates an emotional separation. For Brenda it was as if her mother had repeatedly walked out on her. When Brenda understood that her mother's self-centeredness was a kind of emotional abandonment, she could comprehend the depths of her anger for the first time. She wasn't overreacting; she was having a normal response to an emotional injury. And once Brenda understood where her anger was coming from, she could see herself in a different light. She had been a normal child; she had experienced the anger that any child would feel if a parent walked out or refused to respond.

Sometimes children of emotionally immature parents repress their anger or turn it against themselves. Perhaps they've learned that it's too dangerous to express anger directly, or maybe they feel too guilty about their anger to be aware of it. When anger is internalized in this way, people tend to criticize and blame themselves unrealistically. They may end up severely depressed or even have suicidal feelings—the ultimate expression of anger against the self. Alternatively, some people express their anger in a passive-aggressive way, attempting to defeat their parents and other authority figures with behaviors like forgetting, lying, delaying, or avoiding.

They Communicate by Emotional Contagion

Because emotionally immature people have little awareness of feelings and a limited vocabulary for emotional experiences, they usually act out their emotional needs instead of talking about them. They use a method of communication known as emotional contagion (Hatfield, Rapson, and Le 2007), which gets other people to feel what they're feeling.

Emotional contagion is also how babies and little children communicate their needs. They cry and fuss until their caretakers figure out what's wrong and fix it. Emotional contagion from an upset baby to a concerned adult is galvanizing, motivating a caretaker to do anything necessary to calm the child.

Emotionally immature adults communicate feelings in this same primitive way. As parents, when they're distressed they upset their children and everyone around them, typically with the result that others are willing to do anything to make them feel better. In this role reversal, the child catches the contagion of the parent's distress and feels responsible for making the parent feel better. However, if the upset parent isn't trying to understand his or her own feelings, nothing ever gets resolved. Instead the upsetting feelings just get spread around to others, so that everyone reacts without understanding what is truly the matter.

They Don't Do Emotional Work

Emotionally immature parents don't try to understand the emotional experiences of other people—including their own children. If accused of being insensitive to the needs or feelings of others, they become defensive, saying something along the lines of "Well, you should have said so!" They might add something about not being a mind reader, or they might dismiss the situation by saying the hurt person is overly emotional or too sensitive. However they respond, the message is the same: they can't be expected to make the effort to understand what's going on inside other people.

In her article "Toiling in the Field of Emotion" (2008, 270), psychiatrist Harriet Fraad uses the term emotional labor to describe this effort to understand others: "Emotional labor is the expenditure of time, effort, and energy utilizing brain and muscle to understand and fulfill emotional needs. By emotional needs, I mean the human needs for feeling wanted, appreciated, loved, and cared for. Individuals' emotional needs are often unspoken or unknown/unconscious. Emotional labor often occurs together with physical labor (producing goods or services), but emotional labor differs from physical labor by aiming to produce the specific feelings of being wanted, appreciated, loved, and/or cared for."

She goes on to explain that some people don't always realize they need emotional comforting, since emotional needs are often vague or subconscious. Other people might hide their need because they're ashamed to admit it, so helpers must offer comfort tactfully and obliquely, allowing the person to save face.

Emotional labor is hard work. People doing this work must also keep reading the other person to know if their efforts are effective. Many roles and occupations depend heavily on emotional labor, and if it's done well, others hardly notice the effort involved. Good mothering is an example of this unsung labor, as are any number of service industry professions.

Mature people take on the emotional work in relationships automatically because they live in a state of empathy and self-awareness. It's impossible for them to overlook the fact that someone they care about is having a hard time. Doing this work allows them to successfully navigate all kinds of interpersonal situations without stepping on other people's toes. Both at work and at home, emotional labor promotes goodwill and good relationships.

Emotionally immature people, on the other hand, often take pride in their *lack* of this skill. They rationalize their impulsive and insensitive responses with excuses like "I'm just saying what I think" or "I can't change who I am." If you confront them with the fact that not saying everything you think is a sign of good sense or that people can't mature without changing who they are, they will probably respond with anger or by dismissing you as ridiculous.

It's as though they think they're off the hook if others don't spell out their pain or difficulty in words. They believe that they aren't required to be tuned in to others' feelings. However, emotionally mature people are almost always sensitive to others, knowing this is simply part of having good relationships. For people who have empathy, emotional work flows easily. However, for those who are unskilled at empathy and find other people's minds to be opaque, emotional work doesn't feel natural at all.

This may be one reason why emotionally immature people complain so much when others expect them to make the effort.

They Are Hard to Give To

Emotionally immature people crave attention to their needs, yet they're actually hard to give to. This trait has been called poor receptive capacity by researcher Leigh McCullough (McCullough et al. 2003). Emotionally immature people want others to show concern about their problems, but they aren't likely to accept helpful suggestions. They reflexively reject efforts to make them feel cared about. They pull others in, but when people try to help, they push them away.

In addition, these people seem to expect others to read their minds and are often quick to anger if people don't anticipate their wishes fast enough (McCullough et al. 2003). They dislike having to tell people what they need and instead hold back, waiting to see whether anyone will notice how they're feeling. The classic unspoken demand of the emotionally immature adult is "If you really loved me, you'd know what I want you to do."

As an example, one woman described her mother's habit of sitting in the den and waiting until a family member came back from the kitchen to complain angrily that the person hadn't thought to ask her if she wanted anything. Instead of speaking up about what they need, emotionally immature people create a malignant guessing game that keeps everybody uneasy.

They Resist Repairing Relationships

Problems are bound to come up in any relationship, so it's important to know how to handle conflict in ways that help the relationship weather the storm. It takes confidence and maturity to admit to being wrong and try to make things better. But emotionally immature people resist facing their mistakes.

People who have been wronged by an emotionally immature person may start to think they're at fault if they continue to feel hurt by what the person did. Emotionally immature people expect you to take them off the hook immediately. If it feels better to blame you for not forgiving them fast enough, that's what they'll do.

After a rift, many people will make what relationship expert John Gottman calls a repair attempt (1999), apologizing, asking for forgiveness, or making amends in a way that shows a desire to patch things up. But emotionally immature people have a completely unrealistic idea of what forgiveness means. To them, forgiveness should make it like the rift never happened, as though a completely fresh start is possible. They have no awareness of the need for emotional processing or the amount of time it may take to rebuild trust after a major betrayal. They just want things to be normal again. Others' pain is the only fly in the ointment. Everything would be fine if others would just get past their feelings about the situation.

They Demand Mirroring

Mirroring is a form of empathy and relatedness that mature parents spontaneously give to their children. Sensitive and emotionally responsive parents mirror their children's feelings by showing those same emotions on their faces (Winnicott 1971). They look concerned when their children are sad and display enthusiasm when their children are happy. In this way, sensitive parents teach their children about emotions and how to engage spontaneously with others. Good mirroring from a parent also gives a child the feeling of being known and understood as a unique individual. This isn't the case for the children of emotionally immature parents. As one man said regarding his mother, "She doesn't see me for who I am. She will never know me, even though I'm her own child."

In fact, emotionally immature parents expect their children to know and mirror *them*. They can get highly upset if their children don't act the way they want them to. Their fragile self-esteem rides on things going their way every time. However, no child is psychologically capable of mirroring an adult accurately.

Emotionally immature parents often have the fantasy that their babies will make them feel good about themselves. When their children turn out to have their own needs, it can send such parents into a state of intense anxiety. Those who are extremely emotionally immature may then use punishment, threats of abandonment, and shaming as trump cards in an attempt to feel in control and bolster their self-esteem—at their children's expense.

————Cynthia's Story————

Cynthia's mother, Stella, who was extremely volatile, expected Cynthia to mirror her every mood, like an emotional clone. When Cynthia decided to travel as a young adult, Stella exploded, yelling, "You're disowned!" and broke off all contact with Cynthia. She didn't talk to Cynthia for months, not even on her birthday. Cynthia summed up her mother's message as "You wanted to be on your own. You left me. I don't want anything to do with you."

After another episode of rage, sparked by Cynthia's plan to visit a friend in Canada, Stella cut off Cynthia's college funds. She told Cynthia that she was selfish for wanting to travel, saying, "What's the matter with you? Life isn't about having fun!" Stella could only feel safe if Cynthia mirrored the same kind of narrow life she'd had.

Fortunately, Cynthia had a strong personality. She put herself through college and became a flight attendant, traveling to exotic locations. But in the back of her mind, she still had the belief that if she wanted to keep any relationship, she had to appease and mirror the other person. She told me that she always feared people would react as her mother did, punishing her for daring to be different from them.

Their Self-Esteem Rides on Your Compliance

People who are emotionally immature only feel good about themselves when they can get other people to give them what they want and to act like they think they should. Given this shaky self-worth, it's hard for emotionally immature parents to tolerate their children's emotions. An upset or fussy child can stir up their anxieties about their own fundamental goodness. If they can't immediately calm their child, they may feel like a failure and then blame the child for upsetting them.

For instance, Jeff remembered an incident from childhood when he asked his father for help with homework. When Jeff didn't understand the lesson immediately, his father yelled, "How goddamn stupid can you be? Stop being so lazy! You just don't try." Not surprisingly, Jeff was mortified and didn't ask for help again. What he couldn't understand as a child was that his father was fighting his own terror of being an incompetent father if he failed to help his son understand easily and immediately. His reaction wasn't about Jeff at all.

For emotionally immature people, all interactions boil down to the question of whether they're good people or bad ones, which explains their extreme defensiveness if you try to talk to them about something they did. They often respond to even mild complaints about their behavior with an extreme statement, like "Well, then, I must be the worst mother ever!" or "Obviously I can't do anything right!" They would rather shut down communication than hear something that could make them feel like bad people.

They See Roles as Sacred

If there's anything emotionally immature people are keen on in relationships, it's role compliance. Roles simplify life and make decisions clear-cut. As parents, emotionally immature people need their children to play a proper role that includes respecting and obeying them. They often use platitudes to support the authority of their role as a parent because, like roles, platitudes oversimplify complex situations and make them easier to deal with.

Role Entitlement

Role entitlement is an attitude of demanding certain treatment because of your social role. When parents feel entitled to do what they want simply because they're in the role of parent, this is a form of role entitlement. They act as though being a parent exempts them from respecting boundaries or being considerate.

Mardi's parents provide a classic example of role entitlement. Mardi and her husband moved to a different city after Mardi's husband was transferred. Not long afterward, Mardi's parents moved nearby. Once in the neighborhood, her parents began stopping by unannounced and even walked into her house without knocking. When Mardi suggested that they call first, her parents were indignant and cited their roles as parents to claim their right to drop in anytime.

Here's another example: Faith had to ban visits from her mother, a real estate agent, because she insisted on making changes to the furniture and accessories in Faith's house. Even after Faith told her mother to stop, she protested that she should be allowed to do it because she was Faith's mother and a realtor—two key roles for her.

Role Coercion

Role coercion occurs when people insist that someone live out a role because they want them to. As parents, they try to force their children into acting a certain way by not speaking to them, threatening to reject them, or getting other family members to gang up against them. Role coercion often involves a heavy dose of shame and guilt, such as telling a child that he or she is a bad person for wanting something the parent disapproves of.

My client Jillian, whose family was rigidly religious, experienced a malignant case of role coercion. Jillian married an abusive man who physically injured her numerous times. She finally found the courage to leave him, only to have her mother insist that she return to her husband. Desperate for her mother's support, Jillian finally told her mother about the abuse. But in her mother's eyes, that was beside the point; Jillian now held the role of a married woman, and divorce was a sin.

In another example, when Mason told his mother he thought he might be gay, she said he couldn't be, "because you are not a zebra." In her mind, the role of her son was firmly heterosexual, and if her son didn't see himself that way, he was as deluded as if he were claiming he was a different species.

Insistence on complying with roles to this degree is a profound invalidation of a child's most personal and essential choices in life. Yet emotionally immature parents have no qualms about doing it because they aren't comfortable with complexity and prefer life simplified. In their view, not fulfilling a supposed role means something is wrong with a person and the person needs to change.

They Seek Enmeshment, Not Emotional Intimacy

Although emotional intimacy and enmeshment can look superficially similar, these two styles of interaction are very different. In emotional intimacy, two individuals with fully articulated selves enjoy getting to know each other at a deep level, building emotional trust through mutual acceptance. In the process of getting to know each other, they discover and even cherish differences between them. Emotional intimacy is invigorating and energizes people toward personal growth as they enjoy the interest and support of another person.

In enmeshment, on the other hand, two emotionally immature people seek their identity and self-completion through an intense, dependent relationship (Bowen 1978). Through this enmeshed relationship, they create a sense of certainty, predictability, and security that relies on the reassuring familiarity of each person playing a comfortable role for the other. If one person tries to step out of the implicit bounds of the relationship, the other often experiences great anxiety that's only eased by a return to the prescribed role.

Playing Favorites

Enmeshment sometimes manifests as playing favorites (Libby 2010). It can be hard to watch your parent give attention to a preferred sibling, making you wonder why your parent never showed that kind of interest in you. But obvious favoritism isn't a sign of a close relationship; it's a sign of enmeshment. It's likely that the preferred sibling has a psychological maturity level similar to your parent's (Bowen 1978). Low levels of emotional maturity pull people into mutual enmeshment, especially if they are parent and child.

Remember, emotionally immature parents relate on the basis of roles, not individuality. If you had an independent, self-reliant personality, your parent wouldn't have seen you as a needy child for whom he or she could play the role of rescuing parent. Instead, you may have been pegged as the child without needs, the little grown-up. It wasn't some sort of insufficiency in you that made your parent pay more attention to your sibling; rather, it's likely that you weren't dependent enough to trigger your parent's enmeshment instincts.

Interestingly, self-sufficient children who don't spur their parents to become enmeshed are often left alone to create a more independent and self-determined life (Bowen 1978). Therefore, they can achieve a level of self-development exceeding that of their parents. In this way, *not* getting attention can actually pay off in the long run. But in the meantime, high-functioning children still have the pain of feeling left out as their parent pours energy into emotional enmeshment with one or more siblings.

Enmeshment can take the form of either dependency or idealization. In dependent enmeshment, the child is maladjusted and the parent plays the role of either rescuer or victim. In idealized enmeshment, the parent indulges a favorite child as though that child is more important and deserving than the other kids. However, this traps the idealized favorite child in an ironclad role, so that child isn't experiencing any true emotional intimacy either.

———Heather's Story———

Heather had always longed for her mother's interest and attention but had never received it, while her eldest sister, Marlo, was the clear favorite. Heather was particularly hurt when her mother enthusiastically reported how, on a recent visit, she and Marlo had just "talked and talked and talked!"

"About what?" Heather asked.

"Oh, just what she was doing and what she wants to do."

Heather's heart felt pierced because she had always wished for those kinds of conversations with her mother but it had never happened.

Another time, at a holiday gathering, Heather watched with dismay as her mother fluttered around Marlo with an adoring look, and volunteered to sit on an uncomfortable chair so Marlo could have a nice seat.

Mark's Story

Mark's father, Don, clearly preferred Mark's younger brother, Brett, helping him financially and calling him his baby. When Mark's father died, at the funeral Mark's uncle remembered how hard Don had been on Mark, punishing him harshly for no good reason. "You were the best one," his uncle told him, "I couldn't understand why he was so tough on you." Mark was an independent, intelligent child who was never dependent on his father. They couldn't enmesh, so Don turned to Brett, who was more emotionally immature.

Finding Substitute Family Members

Emotionally immature parents can act out their need for enmeshment even with people who aren't close family members. If there's an enmeshment void, they'll go outside the immediate family to fill it. They might also become enmeshed with a group, such as a church or other organization.

Bill's Story

After Bill was grown and out of the house, his parents started taking in homeless people they met through a church outreach program. At any get-together, Bill's parents would regale people with stories about the latest in the lives of the people they were helping. Although Bill's parents were very invested in talking about the latest person they had taken under their wings, they rarely mentioned anything Bill was involved in.

63

They Have an Inconsistent Sense of Time

Although this is an extremely subtle point and easily overlooked, emotionally immature people often have a fragmented orientation to time, especially when they get emotional. We might assume that all adults experience time in the same way, using a kind of linear continuum that stretches seamlessly from the distant past into the foreseeable future. Not so with emotionally immature people. When they get emotionally aroused, moments exist in a kind of eternal *now*. This is one reason why the lives of emotionally immature people are often beset with problems: they don't see them coming. Ruled by desires of the moment, their experiences in time are frequently disconnected. When acting on their impulses, they don't use the past for guidance, and they don't anticipate the future. This disturbance in time continuity explains their inconsistencies and the unreflective way they handle relationship issues.

Why a Poor Sense of Time Can Look Like Emotional Manipulation

Emotionally immature people may seem to be emotional manipulators, but actually they're just very opportunistic tacticians, pressing for whatever feels best at the time. They have no investment in being consistent, so they say whatever gives them an edge in the moment. They may be capable of strategic thinking in their work or in other pursuits, but when it comes to emotional situations, they go for the immediate advantage. Lying is a perfect example of a momentary win that feels good but is destructive to a relationship in the long run.

How Lacking a Sense of Time's Continuity Creates Inconsistency

When stressed or emotionally aroused, immature people don't experience themselves as being embedded in the ongoing flow of time. They experience moments in time as separate, nonlinear blips, like little lights randomly going on and off, with few linkages in time between one interaction and another. They act inconsistently, as their consciousness hops from one experience to another. This is one reason why they're often indignant when you remind them of their past behavior. For them, the past is gone and has nothing to do with the present. Likewise, if you express caution about something in the future, they're likely to brush you off, since the future isn't here yet.

More emotionally mature people, on the other hand, experience time as a series of connected, self-aware moments. If they regret something they did, it continues to travel through time with them, attached to them by an emotion like shame or guilt. If they think about doing something risky in the future, they feel linked to what might happen and may choose to do something different. The moments of their lives feel connected, each affecting the others, and all affecting their relationships with other people.

How an Immature Sense of Time Limits Self-Reflection and Accountability

Self-reflection is the ability to analyze your thoughts, feelings, and behaviors over time. People who focus mostly on the present moment don't have enough of a time perspective to engage in self-reflection. Instead, with each new moment they leave their past behind, freeing them from any sense of responsibility for their actions. Therefore, when someone feels hurt by something they did in the past, they tend to accuse the person of dwelling on the past for no good reason. They don't understand why others can't just forgive, forget, and move on. Because of their limited sense of the continuity of time, they don't understand that it takes time to heal from a betrayal.

You can see how hard accountability would be for these people; it's a flimsy concept for those who don't feel a temporal connection between their actions and future consequences. As a result, their natural style is to promise something, not do it, apologize perfunctorily, and then resent people if they keep bringing it up. You may wonder why a person would develop such an unreliable sense of time, being blind to their own inconsistencies and unable to observe their own behavior. It has to do with their lack of self-development and poor personality integration, along with their tendency toward extremely concrete, literal thinking. Because they don't have an ongoing, continuous self as the organizing center of their personality, emotions or stress can put them in a childlike mentality in which moments in time float separately.

Summary

Emotionally immature people have a poor sense of personal history and resist being accountable for their past actions or future consequences. Lacking a firm sense of self, they think family closeness means enmeshment, with people existing to mirror each other. Real communication is nearly impossible because of their poor empathy and rigid emphasis on roles. They neglect relationship repair and reciprocity and shirk the emotional work necessary to be sensitive to other people. Instead, they focus on whether others seem to make them look good or bad. Defending against anxiety trumps relating authentically to other people, including their children.

In the next chapter, we'll take a look at some of the research on early mother-child attachment to see how these immature characteristics might arise. Then I'll discuss how this translates into four main types of emotionally immature parents.

Chapter 4

Four Types of
Emotionally
Immature Parents

T here are different types of emotionally immature parents, but all can cause loneliness and insecurity in children. There's basically one way to provide nurturing love, but many ways to frustrate a child's need for love. In this chapter, we'll look at four different types of parents, each with a particular brand of emotional immaturity. Although each type is emotionally insensitive in a different way, all create emotional insecurity in their children.

Despite their different styles, all four types have the same underlying emotional immaturity. All tend to be self-involved, narcissistic, and emotionally unreliable. All share the common traits of egocentricity, insensitivity, and a limited capacity for genuine emotional intimacy. All use nonadaptive coping mechanisms that distort reality rather than dealing with it (Vaillant 2000). And all use their children to try to make themselves feel better, often leading to a parent-child role reversal and exposing their children to adult issues in an overwhelming way.

In addition, all four types have poor resonance with other people's feelings. They have extreme boundary problems, either getting too involved or refusing to get involved at all. Most tolerate frustration poorly and use emotional tactics or threats rather than verbal communication to get what they want. All four types of parents resist seeing their children as separate individuals and instead relate to them strictly on the basis of their own needs. And with all four styles, children end up feeling "de-selfed" (Bowen 1978) because their needs and interests are eclipsed by what's important to their parents. Before we explore the four types, however, let's take a brief moment to look at previous research that studied the effects of different types of parenting on quality of attachment behavior in babies.

How Different Types of Parenting Affect Infant Attachment

Mary Ainsworth, Silvia Bell, and Donelda Stayton (1971, 1974) conducted famous infant attachment research that has been replicated many times over the years. Part of their research involved observing and identifying maternal characteristics that were associated with either secure or insecure attachment behaviors in babies. As summarized in their 1974 article, these researchers rated mothers' behaviors toward their babies on four dimensions: sensitivity-insensitivity, acceptance-rejection, cooperation-interference, and accessible-ignoring. They found that a mother's "degree of sensitivity" was "a key variable, in the sense that mothers who rated high in sensitivity also, without exception, rated high in acceptance, cooperation and accessibility, whereas mothers who rated low in any one of the other three scales also rated low in sensitivity" (1974, 107). Ainsworth and her colleagues reported that more sensitive mothers had babies who showed more secure attachment behaviors in their experiments.

Here's how these researchers described the sensitive mothers of babies who showed secure attachment behaviors: "In summary, highly sensitive mothers are usually accessible to their infants and are aware of even their more subtle communications, signals, wishes, and moods; in addition, these mothers accurately interpret their perceptions and show empathy with their infants. The sensitive mother, armed with this understanding and empathy, can time her interactions well and deal with her baby so that her interactions seem appropriate—appropriate in kind as well as in quality—and prompt" (1974, 131).

However, the behaviors of mothers who had babies showing insecure attachment behaviors were very different. Thinking back to chapters 2 and 3 of this book, see if the following description of insensitive mothers, from Mary Ainsworth and her colleagues, reminds you of characteristics of what I am calling emotionally immature parents:

> In contrast, mothers with low sensitivity are not aware of much of their infant's behaviour either because they ignore the baby or they fail to perceive in his activity the more subtle and hard-to-detect communications. Furthermore, insensitive mothers often do not understand those aspects of their infant's behaviour of which they are aware or else they distort it. A mother may have somewhat accurate perceptions of her infant's activity and moods but may be unable to empathise with him. Through either lack of understanding or empathy, mothers with low sensitivity improperly time their responses, either in terms of scheduling or in terms of promptness to the baby's communications. Further, mothers with low sensitivity often have inappropriate responses in kind as well as in quantity, i.e interactions which are fragmented and poorly resolved. (Ainsworth, Bell, and Stayton 1974, 131)

These research findings support the idea that a mother's levels of sensitivity and empathy strongly affect the quality of the baby's attachment behaviors in the mother-child relationship.

The Four Types of Emotionally Immature Parents

Keeping in mind this previous research on infant attachment, let's now take a look at what I've categorized as the four main types of emotionally immature parents, who are all especially likely to create feelings of insecurity in their children. Although each type undermines a child's emotional security in different ways, all of them relate to their children with limited empathy and unreliable emotional support, and their fundamental lack of sensitivity is the same. Also, be aware that each type exists along a continuum, from mild to severe, with varying degrees of narcissism. In severe cases, the parent may be mentally ill or physically or sexually abusive.

- **Emotional parents** are run by their feelings, swinging between overinvolvement and abrupt withdrawal. They are prone to frightening instability and unpredictability. Overwhelmed by anxiety, they rely on others to stabilize them. They treat small upsets like the end of the world and see other people as either rescuers or abandoners.

- **Driven parents** are compulsively goal-oriented and super busy. They can't stop trying to perfect everything, including other people. Although they rarely pause long enough to have true empathy for their children, they are controlling and interfering when it comes to running their children's lives.

- **Passive parents** have a laissez-faire mind-set and avoid dealing with anything upsetting. They're less obviously harmful than the other types but have their own negative effects. They readily take a backseat to a dominant mate, even allowing abuse and neglect to occur by looking the other way. They cope by minimizing problems and acquiescing.

- **Rejecting parents** engage in a range of behaviors that make you wonder why they have a family in the first place. Whether their behavior is mild or severe, they don't enjoy emotional intimacy and clearly don't want to be bothered by children. Their tolerance for other people's needs is practically nil, and their interactions consist of issuing commands, blowing up, or isolating themselves from family life. Some of the milder types may engage in stereotyped family activities, but they still show little closeness or real engagement. They mostly want to be left alone to do their thing.

As you read the following descriptions, keep in mind that some parents are a blend of types. While most parents tend to fall into one category, any may be prone to behaviors that fit a different type when under certain kinds of stress. And within the following descriptions, you'll see a unifying thread: none of the types are able to consistently act in ways that would make a child feel secure about the relationship. However, each type has its own unique way of falling short. Also, note that my purpose here is just to provide an outline of the four parenting types. I'll discuss the best ways of dealing with emotionally immature parents in later chapters.

The Emotional Parent

Emotional parents are the most infantile of the four types. They give the impression that they need to be watched over and handled carefully. It doesn't take much to upset them, and then everyone in the family scrambles to soothe them. When emotional parents disintegrate, they take their children with them into their personal meltdown. Their children experience their despair, rage, or hatred in all its intensity. It's no wonder that everyone in the family feels like they're walking on eggshells. These parents' emotional instability is the most predictable thing about them.

At the severe end of the spectrum, these parents are, quite frankly, mentally ill. They may be psychotic or bipolar, or have narcissistic or borderline personality disorder. At times, their unbridled emotionality can even result in suicide attempts or physical attacks on others. People are nervous around them because their emotions can escalate so quickly, and because it's so frightening to see someone you know come unglued. Suicide threats are especially terrifying to children, who feel the crushing burden of trying to keep their parent alive but don't know what to do. At the milder end of the spectrum, emotional instability is the biggest issue, perhaps in the form of histrionic personality disorder or a cyclothymic disorder, characterized by alternating episodes of high and low mood.

Regardless of severity, all such parents have difficulty tolerating stress and emotional arousal. They lose their emotional balance and behavioral control in situations mature adults could handle. Of course, substance abuse may make them even more unbalanced and unable to tolerate frustration or distress.

Whatever their degree of self-control, these parents are governed by emotion, seeing the world in black-and-white terms, keeping score, holding grudges, and controlling others with emotional tactics. Their fluctuating moods and reactivity make them unreliable and intimidating. And while they may act helpless and usually see themselves as victims, family life always revolves around their moods. Although they often control themselves outside the family, where they can follow a structured role, within the crucible of intimate family relationships they display their full impulsivity, especially if intoxicated. It can be shocking to see how no-holds-barred they can get.

Many children of such parents learn to subjugate themselves to other people's wishes (Young and Klosko 1993). Because they grew up anticipating their parent's stormy emotional weather, they can be overly attentive to other people's feelings and moods, often to their own detriment.

———Brittany's Story———

Despite the fact that Brittany was in her forties and living independently, her mother, Shonda, still tried to control Brittany with her emotions. Once, when Brittany was in bed sick for several days, Shonda's anxiety mounted until she called Brittany five times in one day. She also stopped by because she thought it was time for Brittany to get out of bed, even though Brittany had asked her not to come over. Finally, Brittany latched the screen door so Shonda couldn't get in. Later, Shonda told her, "When you locked me out, I was so angry that I wanted to break your door down!" When confronted about her intrusiveness, Shonda acted wounded and hid behind the excuse "I just needed to know you're better." But the truth was, her primary concern was with her own feelings, not with what Brittany needed.

The Driven Parent

Driven parents are the type that tends to look most normal, even appearing exceptionally invested in their children's lives. Being driven, they're always focused on getting things done. Whereas emotional parents are obvious in their immaturity, driven parents seem so invested in their child's success that their egocentrism is hard to see. Most of the time, you wouldn't notice anything unhealthy about them. However, their children may have trouble with either initiative or self-control. Paradoxically, these very involved, hardworking parents often end up with unmotivated, even depressive children.

If you look a bit deeper, you can detect the emotional immaturity in these upstanding, responsible people. It shows up in the way they make assumptions about other people, expecting everyone to want and value the same things they do. Their excessive self-focus manifests as a conviction that they know what's "good" for others.

They don't experience self-doubt at a conscious level and prefer to pretend that everything is settled and they already have the answers. Rather than accepting their children's unique interests and life paths, they selectively praise and push what they want to see. Their frequent interference in their children's lives is legendary. In addition, their worry about getting enough done runs them like a motor. Goals take precedence over the feelings of others, including their children.

Driven parents usually grew up in an emotionally depriving environment. They learned to get by on their own efforts rather than expecting to be nurtured. Often self-made, they're proud of their independence. They fear that their children will embarrass them by not succeeding, yet they can't offer their children the unconditional acceptance that would give them a secure foundation from which to go out and achieve.

Whether they mean to or not, driven parents make their children feel evaluated constantly. An example would be a father who makes his kids practice the piano in front of him so he can point out their mistakes. This kind of excessive oversight often sours children on seeking adult help for anything. As a result, in adulthood they may resist connecting with potential mentors.

Certain they know the best way to do things, driven parents sometimes do outlandish things. One mother insisted on going to her adult daughter's house to pay her bills because she was sure her daughter wouldn't do it right. Another mother bought her adult son a used car he hadn't asked for and was hurt when he didn't want it. And one young man's father made his son weigh himself every day in front of him when he gained weight.

If you think back to the infant attachment studies described at the beginning of this chapter (Ainsworth, Bell, and Stayton 1971, 1974), driven parents seem similar to some of the emotionally insensitive mothers of insecurely attached babies. Out of sync with their child's moment-to-moment experience, they don't adapt themselves to their child's needs; instead, they push their child toward what they think he or she should be doing. As a result, the children of driven parents always feel they should be doing more, or be doing something other than whatever they are doing.

John's Story

Although John was twenty-one, he spent a lot of time with his parents and didn't feel any ownership of his life. Describing how he felt around his mother, he said, "I'm constantly on her radar." John felt so pressured by his parents' hopes for him that he'd lost all confidence in his own ideas for his future.

As he put it, "I worry so much about what they expect from me, I have no idea what I want. I'm just trying to keep my parents happy and off my case." This was especially true on family vacations, when John felt that his father got really angry if John wasn't having a good enough time.

John's parents were so overinvolved in his life that he was afraid to set any goals, since that seemed to make them even pushier about what he needed to do next. They were killing his initiative by always urging him to do a bit more or try a little harder. At a conscious level, they wanted the best for John, but they were tone-deaf when it came to respecting and fostering his autonomy.

Christine's Story

Christine was an attorney with a very domineering father, Joseph, who constantly pushed her to be a success. Early in our work together, she described her childhood like this: "My father controlled me. He couldn't stand anyone having a different opinion; it was absolutely intolerable to him. I was so afraid of making the wrong choice that I made a lot of decisions based on fear. It was as if my father completely owned me. Even in college I had to be home by eleven, which was extremely embarrassing, but I wouldn't have dreamed of challenging him."

Joseph even tried to control Christine's thoughts. If Christine came up with an idea her father didn't like, his response was immediate: "Don't even *think* about it!"

Joseph also had lack of empathy that made him a terrible teacher. He couldn't sense what might be terrifying to a child, so he tried to teach Christine to swim by literally dropping her in a pool. As Christine put it, "He would command me to do well but didn't offer any guidance or help. I was simply ordered to be a success." To all outward appearances, Christine did become a success, but on the inside she felt a tremendous insecurity, like she didn't really know what she was doing.

The Passive Parent

Passive parents aren't angry or pushy like the other three types, but they still have negative effects. They passively acquiesce to dominant personalities and often partner with more intense types who are also immature, which makes sense given that people with similar emotional maturity levels are attracted to one another (Bowen 1978).

Compared to the other types, these parents seem more emotionally available, but only up to a point. When things get too intense, they become passive, withdraw emotionally, and hide their heads in the sand. They don't offer their children any real limits or guidance to help them navigate the world. They may love you, but they can't help you.

Passive parents are as immature and self-involved as the other types, but their easygoing and often playful ways make them much more lovable than the other three types (emotional, driven, or rejecting). They are often the favorite parent and can show some empathy for their children, as long as doing so doesn't get in the way of their needs. And because they can be as egocentric as the other types, passive parents may use their child to meet their own emotional needs—primarily their need to be the focus of someone's affectionate attention. They enjoy the child's innocent openness and can get on the child's level in a delightful way. The child loves his or her time with this parent—but because the child is often filling the parent's need for an admiring, attentive companion, it becomes a kind of emotional incest. This kind of relationship is never completely comfortable for the child because it poses the risk of making the other parent jealous, and may even feel sexualized.

Children wisely know not to expect or ask for much help from these parents. While passive parents often enjoy their children, have fun with them, and make them feel special, the children sense that their parents aren't really there for them in any essential way. In fact, these parents are famous for turning a blind eye to family situations that are harmful to their children, leaving their kids to fend for themselves. When the mother is the passive parent, she may stay with a partner who demeans or abuses her children because she doesn't have an independent income. Such mothers often numb themselves to what's going on around them. For example, one mother later referred to her husband's violent attacks on their children with the mild statement "Daddy could be tough sometimes."

In their own upbringing, passive parents often learned to stay out of the line of fire, keeping a low profile and subjugating themselves to stronger personalities. As adults, it doesn't occur to them that they have a mission not only to have fun with their own children, but to protect them. Instead, they go into a kind of trance during the worst times, retreating into themselves or finding other passive ways to weather the storm.

In addition to unthinkingly abandoning their children when the going gets rough, these parents may leave the family if they get a chance at a happier life. If the passive but more emotionally connected parent leaves the family for any reason, the wound to the child can be especially deep, since the abandonment came from the parent who meant the most to the child.

Children who adored a passive parent can become adults who make excuses for other people's abandoning behavior. As children, they believed nothing could be done about their childhood situation and that the passive parent was truly helpless. They're often taken aback by the idea that their wonderful, nice parent actually had a responsibility to stand up for them when they couldn't protect themselves as children. They've never considered that parents have a duty to put their children's emotional welfare at least on an even footing with their own interests.

Molly's Story

Molly's mother was a short-tempered, physically abusive woman who worked long hours and usually came home in a foul mood. Her father was a sweet, affectionate man who was usually in good spirits. He was fond of puttering in the garage when he wasn't at work, so Molly was mostly left in the care of her abusive, demeaning older sister, apparently with no consideration of how Molly might be treated.

Molly's safe haven was her relationship with her father. His kindness was the single bright spot and source of love in her life, and she both worshipped him and felt protective of him. It never occurred to her to expect him to protect her. For example, once when her mother flew into a rage and was beating Molly in the den, she heard her father banging pots around in the kitchen. She interpreted this as his way of letting her know he was still there for her. She had no expectation that he should step in and stop the abuse. This is a poignant example of how emotionally deprived children try to put a positive spin on their favorite parent's behavior no matter what.

Molly also had a slight stutter, and one time on a trip to an amusement park, Molly's sister and her friends teased Molly about it so much that she became hysterical. Molly's father laughed it off, rather than admonishing the older kids or attending to Molly's feelings. On the drive home, everyone laughed uproariously as they took turns imitating Molly's speech impediment.

The Rejecting Parent

Rejecting parents seem to have a wall around them. They don't want to spend time with their children and seem happiest if others leave them alone to do what they want. Their children get the feeling the parent would be fine if they didn't exist. These parents' irritated demeanor teaches their children not to approach them, something one person described as running toward someone only to have the door slammed in her face. They summarily reject attempts to draw them into affectionate or emotional interactions. If pushed for a response, they may become angry or even abusive. These parents are capable of punitive physical attacks.

Rejecting parents are also the least empathic of the four types. They often use avoidance of eye contact to signal their distaste for emotional intimacy or sometimes employ a blank look or hostile stare designed to make others go away.

These parents rule the home, with family life revolving around their wishes. A well-known example of this type is the aloof and scary father—a man with no emotional warmth for his children. Everything revolves around him, and the family instinctively tries to not upset him. With a rejecting father, it's easy to feel apologetic for existing. But mothers can be rejecting too.

Children of rejecting parents come to see themselves as bothers and irritants, causing them to give up easily, whereas more secure children tend to keep making requests or complaining to get what they want. This can have serious ramifications later in life when, as adults, these rejected children find it hard to ask for what they need.

————Beth's Story————

Beth's mother, Rosa, never showed any enthusiasm about spending time with her. When Beth visited, Rosa resisted hugs and immediately found something to criticize about Beth's appearance. She usually urged Beth to call a relative as soon as Beth walked in the door, as though to redirect her elsewhere. If Beth suggested spending time together, Rosa acted irritated and told Beth she was too dependent on her. When Beth telephoned her mother, anything Beth said was usually cut short as Rosa quickly found an excuse to get off the phone, often giving the phone to Beth's father.

Exercise: Determining Your Parent's Type

To assess which of these four types might fit your parent, read through the following lists and check off the characteristics you associate with your parent, bearing in mind that parents of any type can exhibit traits of the other types when very stressed. Characteristics of emotional immaturity common to all types include self-preoccupation, low empathy, disregard for boundaries, resisting emotional intimacy, poor communication, an absence of self-reflection, refusal to repair relationship problems, emotional reactivity, impulsiveness, and problems sustaining emotional closeness.

As before, if you'd like to complete this assessment for more than one parent or stepparent, use the downloadable version of this exercise available at http://www.newharbinger.com/31700. (See the back of the book for instructions on how to access it. With the downloadable content, you'll also find a table summarizing these traits.)

Emotional Parent

_____ Is preoccupied with his or her own needs

_____ Has low empathy

_____ Is enmeshed and not respectful of boundaries

_____ Is defensively nonintimate

_____ Doesn't engage in reciprocal communication; just talks about himself or herself

_____ Isn't self-reflective

_____ Has poor relationship repair skills

_____ Is reactive, not thoughtful

_____ Is either too close or too distant

_____ Blows up or cuts others off

_____ Has frightening or intimidating emotional intensity

_____ Expects his or her child to provide soothing and doesn't think about the child's needs

_____ Likes to pretend he or she doesn't run the show

_____ Sees himself or herself as a victim

Driven Parent

_____ Is preoccupied with his or her own needs

_____ Has low empathy

_____ Is enmeshed and not respectful of boundaries

_____ Is defensively nonintimate

_____ Doesn't engage in reciprocal communication; just talks about himself or herself

_____ Isn't self-reflective

_____ Has poor relationship repair skills

_____ Is reactive, not thoughtful

_____ Is either too close or too distant

_____ Has rigid values and perfectionistic expectations

_____ Is goal-obsessed and busy, with machinelike tunnel vision

_____ Sees his or her child as a reflection, without considering what the child wants

_____ Likes to run the show

_____ Sees himself or herself as a fixer

Passive Parent

_____ Is preoccupied with his or her own needs

_____ Has limited empathy

_____ Is enmeshed and not respectful of boundaries

_____ Can be sporadically emotionally intimate

_____ Engages only minimally in reciprocal communication; mostly talks about himself or herself

_____ Isn't self-reflective

_____ Has limited relationship repair skills

_____ Can be thoughtful on occasion

_____ Is either too close or too distant

_____ Can be kindly and fun but not protective

_____ Has a laissez-faire attitude that all is well

_____ Is affectionate toward the child but doesn't stand up for him or her

_____ Likes someone else to run the show or be the bad guy

_____ Sees himself or herself as mellow and good-natured

Rejecting Parent

_____ Is preoccupied with his or her own needs

_____ Shows no empathy

_____ Has impenetrable boundaries

_____ Seems disconnected and hostile

_____ Seldom engages in communication

_____ Isn't self-reflective

_____ Has no relationship repair skills

_____ Is reactive, attacking, and demeaning

_____ Is too distant

_____ Ignores his or her child or can be rageful toward the child

_____ Is often rejecting and angry

_____ Sees his or her child as a bother and doesn't want to get near the child

_____ Likes to mock and dismiss

_____ Sees himself or herself as independent from others

Summary

All four types of emotionally immature parents are self-involved and insensitive and therefore emotionally unavailable to their children. Their lack of empathy makes them hard to communicate with and difficult to connect with. They're all afraid of genuine emotion and seek to control others for their own comfort. None of them make their children feel emotionally seen. All are draining to be around in their own ways, and ultimately all interactions center around them. In addition, all are incapable of true interpersonal reciprocity.

Although there are four general types of emotionally immature parent, their children tend to fall into just two main categories: internalizers and externalizers. In the next chapter, we'll take a look at these two very different coping styles.

Chapter 5

How Different Children React to Emotionally Immature Parenting

When immature parents can't engage emotionally and give their children enough attention or affection, their children cope by imagining healing fantasies about how their unmet emotional needs will be fulfilled in the future. They also cope by finding a special family role, creating what I call a role-self. The role-self is designed to get some kind of attention from a preoccupied parent. In this chapter, we'll begin by looking at healing fantasies and role-selves and then explore two very different coping styles that children use in order to deal with emotional neglect: internalizing or externalizing.

Unfortunately, neither coping style allows a child to fully develop his or her potential. Because of their parents' self-preoccupation, these children are likely to feel that their true selves aren't enough to engage their parents. As a result, they start believing that the only way to be noticed is to become something other than who they really are.

Sadly, the true self, which consists of a child's innate aptitudes and genuine feelings, takes a backseat to what seems necessary to secure a place in the family. Although the true self still exists beneath the surface, it's often squelched by family rules that put the parent's needs first. In chapter 7, we'll look at what happens when the underlying true self resurfaces to wake people up to their real feelings and full potential. But for now, let's look at how healing fantasies and family roles affect people in both childhood and adult life.

The Origins of Healing Fantasies

Having immature parents forces children to adjust to their parents' emotional limitations. Children react to emotionally immature parenting in a number of ways as they attempt to be noticed, cared for, and engaged with. But the one thing all emotionally deprived children have in common is coming up with a fantasy about how they will eventually get what they need.

As children, we make sense of the world by putting together a story that explains our life to us. We imagine what would make us feel better and create what I call a *healing fantasy*—a hopeful story about what will make us truly happy one day.

Children often think the cure for their childhood pain and emotional loneliness lies in finding a way to change themselves and other people into something other than what they really are. Healing fantasies all have that theme. Therefore, everyone's healing fantasy begins with *If only...* For instance, people may think they'd be loved if only they were selfless or attractive enough, or if only they could find a sensitive, selfless partner. Or they may think their life would be healed by becoming famous or extremely rich or making other people afraid of them. Unfortunately, the healing fantasy is a child's solution that comes from a child's mind, so it often doesn't fit adult realities.

But whatever the healing fantasy, it gives a child the optimism to get through a painful upbringing in hopes of a better future. Many people have survived a miserable childhood in this way. The hopeful fantasy of one day being loved and attended to keeps them going.

How Healing Fantasies Affect Adult Relationships

As we grow into adulthood, we secretly expect our closest relationships to make our healing fantasies come true. Our subconscious expectations for other people come straight from this childhood fantasy world. We believe that if we keep at it long enough, we will eventually get people to change. We might think our emotional loneliness will finally be healed by a partner who always thinks of our needs first or a friend who never lets us down. Often these unconscious fantasies are quite self-defeating. For example, one woman secretly believed that if only she could make her depressed father happy, she would finally be free in her own life to do what she wanted. She didn't realize she was already free to live her own life, even if her father stayed miserable.

Another woman was sure she could get the kind of love she longed for from her husband if she did everything he wanted. When he still didn't give her the attention she thought she'd earned, she was furious with him. Her anger covered the anxiety she felt when she realized her healing story wasn't working, even though she'd given it her best shot. Since childhood, she had been sure she could make herself lovable by being a "good" person.

We usually have no idea that we're trying to foist a healing fantasy on someone, but it can be seen in the little tests of love we put people through. It's easier for an outsider to see how unrealistic the fantasy is. Successful marital therapy often involves exposing how people's healing fantasies try to force their partners to give them the loving childhood they always wished for.

Developing a Role-Self

If your parents or caregivers don't adequately respond to your true self in childhood, you'll figure out what you need to do to make a connection. Instead of just being who you are, you'll develop a *role-self*, or pseudo-self (Bowen 1978), that will give you a secure place in your family system. This role-self gradually replaces the spontaneous expression of the true self. This role-self might be based on a belief such as *I'll become so self-sacrificing that other people will praise me and love me.* Or it might take the negative form of *I'll make them pay attention to me one way or the other.*

The process of assuming a role-self is unconscious; nobody sets out to do it deliberately. We create our role-selves gradually, through trial and error as we see the reactions of others. Regardless of whether a role-self seems positive or negative, as children we saw it as the best way to belong. Then, as adults, we tend to keep playing our role in hopes that someone will pay attention to us in the way we wished our parents had.

You may wonder why all children don't make up wonderfully positive role-selves—why so many people are acting out roles of failure, anger, mental disturbance, emotional volatility, or other forms of misery. One answer is that not every child has the inner resources to be successful and self-controlled in interactions with others. Some children's genetics and neurology propel them into impulsive reactivity instead of constructive action.

Another reason negative role-selves arise is that it's common for emotionally immature parents to subconsciously use different children in the family to express unresolved aspects of their *own* role-self and healing fantasies. For instance, one child may be idealized and indulged as the perfect child, while another is tagged as incompetent, always screwing up and needing help.

How Parents Influence Development of the Role-Self

An example of a parent who pressures a child into a role-self would be an insecure mother who reinforces the fears of a clingy, anxious child to give herself a secure role as the center of that child's life. (*Finally, someone really needs me.*) Another example would be a father with unresolved feelings of inadequacy who belittles his son in order to feel strong and capable in comparison. (*I'm the competent one who has to correct everyone else.*) Or perhaps both parents turn a blind eye to their own underlying anger and self-centeredness and see these traits in their child instead. (*We're loving parents, but our kid is mean and disrespectful.*) Few parents consciously intend to undermine their child's future, but their own anxieties may make them see their own negative, undesired qualities in their children (Bowen 1978). This is a powerful psychological defensive reaction that's beyond their conscious control.

As a child, if you found a role that fit your parent's needs like a key in a lock, you probably would have quickly identified with this role-self. In the process, your true self would have become more invisible as you transformed into what your family system needed you to be. This kind of disinvestment from your true self can sabotage your intimate relationships as an adult. You can't forge a deep and satisfying relationship from the position of a role-self. You have to be able to express enough of your true self to give the other person something real to relate to. Without that, the relationship is just playacting between two role-selves.

Another problem with the role-self is that it doesn't have its own source of energy. It has to steal vitality from the true self. Playing a role is much more tiring than just being yourself because it takes a huge effort to be something you are not. And because it's made-up, the role-self is insecure and afraid of being revealed as an imposter.

Playing a role-self usually doesn't work in the long run because it can never completely hide people's true inclinations. Sooner or later, their genuine needs will bubble up. When people decide to stop playing the role and live more from their true self, they can go forward with more lightness and vitality.

Exercise: Identifying Your Healing Fantasy and Role-Self

You'll need two pieces of paper for this exercise. At the top, title one "Healing Fantasy" and the other "Role-Self."

This first part of this exercise will help you explore and identify your own healing fantasy. At the top of your "Healing Fantasy" page, copy and complete the following sentences. Don't think about it too much; just write down what immediately comes to you.

I wish other people were more _____.

Why is it so hard for people to _____?

For a change, I would love someone to treat me like _____.

Maybe one of these days I'll find someone who will _____.

In an ideal world with good people, other people would _____.

Now we'll use a similar process to help you discover your role-self. On your "Role-Self" page, copy and complete the following sentences, again writing down the first thing that comes to mind.

I try hard to be _____.

The main reason people like me is because I _____.

Other people don't appreciate how much I _____.

I always have to be the one who _____.

I've tried to be the kind of person who _____.

After completing the sentences, use the words and ideas from your responses to write two short descriptions, one for your healing fantasy and one for your role self. These descriptions will reveal your secret ideas about how other people should change in order to make you feel valued and how you think you must behave to be loved.

Finally, write a short summary about what it's been like trying to get others to change and how it has felt to play the role-self you've described in this exercise.

Do you want to keep these fantasies and roles, or are you ready to explore and express your true individuality? If you're ready to live more in keeping with your true self, the rest of this book will help you do just that.

Two Styles of Coping with Emotionally Immature Parents

Healing fantasies and role-selves are as unique as the children who invent them. But overall, children with emotionally immature parents cope with emotional deprivation in one of two ways: either internalizing their problems, or externalizing them. Children who are internalizers believe it's up to them to change things, whereas externalizers expect others to do it for them. In some circumstances, a child might hold both beliefs, but most children primarily adopt one coping style or the other as they struggle to get their needs met.

Which style you've adopted is probably more a matter of personality and constitution than choice. And ultimately, both styles are an attempt to get needs met. As people move through life, they may go through periods of being more internalizing or externalizing, but their basic nature is likely to lean more one way than the other. However, the ideal is to balance these two approaches, so that internalizers learn to seek help externally, from others, and externalizers learn to look inside themselves for control.

Internalizers

Internalizers are mentally active and love to learn things. They try to solve problems from the inside out by being self-reflective and trying to learn from their mistakes. They're sensitive and try to understand cause and effect. Seeing life as an opportunity to develop themselves, they enjoy becoming more competent. They believe they can make things better by trying harder, and they instinctively take responsibility for solving problems on their own. Their main sources of anxiety are feeling guilty when they displease others and the fear of being exposed as imposters. Their biggest relationship downfall is being overly self-sacrificing and then becoming resentful of how much they do for others.

Externalizers

Externalizers take action before they think about things. They're reactive and do things impulsively to blow off anxiety quickly. They tend not to be self-reflective, assigning blame to other people and circumstances rather than their own actions. They experience life as a process of trial and error but rarely use their mistakes to learn how to do better in the future. They're firmly attached to the notion that things need to change in the outside world in order for them to be happy, believing that if only other people would give them what they want, their problems would be solved. Their coping style is frequently so self-defeating and disruptive that other people have to step in to repair the damage from their impulsive actions.

Externalizers feel that competent people owe them help and tend to believe that good things have come to other people rather unfairly. Regarding self-image, they either have very low self-confidence or a sense of inflated superiority. They depend on external soothing, which makes them susceptible to substance abuse, addictive relationships, and many forms of immediate gratification. Their main source of anxiety is that they will be cut off from the external sources their security depends upon. Their biggest relationship problems include being attracted to impulsive people and being overly dependent on others for support and stability.

Understanding the Externalizer's Worldview

It's hard to know which coping style has it worse. Internalizers certainly suffer more consciously, but their tendency to blame themselves has the silver lining of eliciting reassurance and support from others. In contrast, externalizers engage in behaviors that often exasperate and anger others, so when they need help, others typically want to keep their distance. However, externalizers usually keep acting up until somebody steps in to help them. Conversely, internalizers may suffer in silence and continue to look just fine, even as they're breaking down inside. Often, people don't offer internalizers assistance because they don't realize they need it.

This book will probably appeal mostly to people who are internalizers because it's designed to help people understand themselves and others, which typically isn't a strong interest of externalizers. Still, it's important for internalizers to understand the worldview of externalizers in order to deal with them more effectively—especially because most emotionally immature parents are externalizers and struggle against reality rather than coping with it. They blame the outside world for their problems, as if reality were at fault. If you think this sounds like the behavior of a young child, you're exactly right.

Externalizing keeps people from growing psychologically, and is therefore associated with emotional immaturity. Internalizing, on the other hand, promotes psychological development through the use of self-reflection. Because I'll cover internalizers in depth in chapter 6, the rest of this chapter discusses various aspects of externalizing.

Externalizers Create a Vicious Cycle of Self-Defeat

Externalizing tends to elicit punishment and rejection. In contrast to well-behaved internalizers, externalizers act out their anxiety, pain, or depression. They do impulsive things to distract themselves from their immediate problems. Although this may help them feel better temporarily, it creates more problems down the road.

When externalizers have to face the consequences of their impulsivity, they're vulnerable to strong but brief feelings of shame and failure. However, they usually use denial to avoid shame, rather than wondering whether or how they might need to change. This lands them in a vicious cycle of impulsivity followed by feelings of failure that prompt still more impulsivity.

As a result, externalizers repeatedly feel brief bursts of low self-worth and a sense of being bad. To avoid total self-hatred, they rid themselves of shame by blaming others and making excuses. This strategy doesn't win them much sympathy—except among fellow externalizers—so they often end up without the emotional support they were seeking.

Externalizers Seek Solutions Outside Themselves

Externalizers don't get a chance to grow or learn from mistakes because they expel stress as soon as it hits. Believing their problems need to be solved by someone else, they look to others to make them feel better, sometimes with a hint of resentment about not being helped sooner. You might picture them as always looking for an external power source to plug into, while internalizers have their batteries included. Of course, sometimes internalizers need a recharge, but they don't routinely make their problems someone else's issue.

Left unchecked, an early externalizing coping style results in emotional immaturity. Most emotionally immature parents have an externalizing coping style. Because they're always looking outside themselves to feel better, externalizers don't work to develop better self-control. They get overwhelmed by emotion and either deny the seriousness of their problems or blame other people. Externalizers think reality should conform to their wishes, whereas more mature people deal with reality and adapt to it (Vaillant 2000).

Externalizing in children promotes emotional dependency and enmeshment with the parent's dynamics (Bowen 1978). Further, emotionally immature parents may indulge an externalizing child because doing so distracts them from their own unresolved issues. When dealing with an out-of-control child, parents don't have time to think about their own pain from the past. Instead, they can take on the role-self of the strong parent helping a weak and dependent child who couldn't get along without them.

Although externalizing children often struggle with behavioral problems, impulsivity, emotional volatility, and even addictions, these ways of acting out have the advantage of making their distress visible. Their pain doesn't stay unseen, as it does with internalizers, though it may be misinterpreted as defiance, opposition, or senseless troublemaking.

Externalizers Exist Along a Continuum of Severity

Externalizing exists along a continuum of severity. At the extreme end are predatory, sociopathic people who see others as resources to exploit, with no regard for their rights or feelings. Milder or quieter externalizers can look like internalizers because they're so nonconfrontational, but they can be identified by their belief that others should change. That said, milder externalizers may be amenable to growth and self-reflection as they get older.

An example of a mild externalizer was a man who came to therapy because he frequently lost control when stressed and shouted at his wife and kids. He had been raised in a rigid family in which he was hit and humiliated if he made a mistake, so he had had plenty of role models for externalizing behavior. However, because he sincerely wanted things to be better at home, he worked hard to accept his wife and children as sensitive people in their own right, who needed to be worked with rather than overpowered.

Mild externalizers can show up in many forms. As mentioned, on the surface they may even seem to be internalizers. The key is whether they blame others for their unhappiness, as in the next story.

Rodney's Story

On the surface, Rodney seemed to be an empathic internalizer who tried to keep everybody happy. He allowed his wife, Sasha, to tell him what he could and couldn't do, giving her full veto power over his activities. He came to therapy because he was depressed and felt he had lost himself. He was afraid of making Sasha mad and never challenged her because he feared she would leave him. Outwardly, he declared himself responsible for his choices, but he secretly blamed Sasha for restricting his life. In true externalizing fashion, he saw her as controlling his happiness and unhappiness and felt that he wasn't free to do what he wanted without her permission.

Rodney had grown up with an overbearing mother who didn't give him much real nurturance, and as an adult he still saw himself in the role of an overpowered child, now controlled by Sasha. In one therapy session, he pictured himself as a prisoner, a man in chains—a highly externalizing image!

Rodney's wasn't flamboyantly demanding like many externalizers, but just the same, he believed the solutions to his problems were up to someone else. Until he began to recognize this dynamic, he remained just as stuck in his problems as a more severe externalizer. Fortunately, after being in therapy awhile, Rodney saw what he'd been doing and began to speak up for himself. Sasha had no idea he was so upset; she had simply been taking the lead because Rodney never expressed his wishes.

Externalizers Can Be Abusive Siblings

Many of my clients who are internalizers have lived with out-of-control, externalizing siblings. These clients all had the same situation: a predatory, indulged sibling—whether older or younger—made life miserable for them as children while their parents did nothing to intervene. If the sibling was bored or upset, he or she took it out on the client. Their parents often saw the externalizing siblings as special in some way and let them get away with all kinds of bad behavior. In some cases, this even took the form of sexual abuse, which my clients either didn't report because they thought their parents wouldn't believe them or did report, only to have their parents defend the abusive sibling.

Externalizing siblings can also perpetrate emotional abuse, ruling the family with their troubles and tantrums. While the internalizers felt like they couldn't get away with anything, their externalizing siblings were let off the hook repeatedly. Emotionally immature parents often placate or rescue externalizing children. Often this seems like the only solution because the externalizers keep making impulsive choices that make their lives unmanageable.

In a family with an externalizing sibling, the parents' attitude is often to silence any complaints of unfairness by the internalizer, telling the child to try to get along or to understand the sibling's problem. For the parent, nothing is worth getting a kid who externalizes upset. The message to internalizers is that they should put their needs on a back burner and instead focus on what the externalizer needs.

Externalizers are also prone to wrongly accusing others of abuse, presenting themselves as the wronged victim who needs special attention. One innocent woman was shocked when her younger brother, an externalizer, accused her of sexually abusing him in childhood. When he was little, she had sacrificed much of her teen life taking care of him because their parents were focused on a chronically ill grandparent. Her brother's unfounded accusation fit his pattern of casting about for external reasons why he couldn't manage his life. Their parents sided with him immediately, even after my client swore that nothing had happened. The roles her parents and brother played as rescuers and hapless victim were too well-established for the facts to have a bearing.

The Continuum of Coping: Mixed Styles

Like everything in human nature, personality characteristics don't occur in pure forms. Rather, any given trait exists along a continuum. Internalizing and externalizing occur on a spectrum, with the most severe examples of each differing profoundly from one another.

Under the right conditions, each type can display behaviors and attitudes ordinarily associated with the other type. For instance, once externalizers hit rock bottom, they sometimes open up to the idea that they may need to change instead of expecting the world to adjust to them. And when under severe stress, some internalizers start reacting as impulsively as any externalizer.

Externalizers Can Become More Internalizing

Ultimately, externalizing and internalizing are just two sides of being human. Everyone can show more or less of either style depending on circumstances and where they fall on the continuum. That said, people who seek therapy or enjoy reading about self-help are far more likely to have an internalizing style of coping. They are always trying to figure out what they can do to change their lives for the better.

In contrast, people who externalize their problems are more likely to end up in treatment due to external pressures, such as courts, marital ultimatums, or rehab. Much of addiction recovery is geared toward nudging externalizers toward adopting a more internalizing coping style and taking responsibility for themselves. You could even think of groups like AA as a movement designed to turn externalizers into internalizers who become accountable for their own change.

Internalizers Can Externalize When Under Stress

On the other hand, internalizers can slip into externalizing when they get overly stressed or lonely. Sometimes overly self-sacrificing internalizers start acting out their distress through affairs or superficial sexual liaisons. They often feel tremendous shame and guilt about this and are terrified that they'll be found out, yet they're attracted to these liaisons as an escape from an emotionally or sexually barren life. Having an affair helps them feel alive and special again and offers the possibility of getting their needs for attention met outside of their primary relationship without rocking the boat. Most of the time, they first try to talk to their partner about their unhappiness, since their instinct is to take responsibility for solving problems. But if their partner doesn't listen or, worse, rebuffs these overtures, internalizers may go on the lookout for someone to save them—a classic externalizer approach.

Maybe this helps explain many midlife crises, wherein previously responsible people seem to reverse some of their values in surprising ways. They seem to suddenly reject obligations and responsibilities as they seek a more personally rewarding life. But in light of the typical internalizer profile, perhaps the midlife metamorphosis isn't so sudden or surprising after all; maybe it's a result of years of self-denial, followed by the internalizer's realization that other people's needs have come first way too many times.

Substance abuse is another way that internalizers can adopt an externalizing solution under stress, as you can see in the following story.

Ron's Story

Ron was a lifelong internalizer with chronic back pain who constantly tried to please his self-involved mother and critical boss. He originally came to therapy with an internalizer's perspective, looking for ways he could change his life. But as work stresses increased and he began to feel the loneliness and lack of support in his life, he started externalizing by taking more pain medication and drinking more. Finally, Ron confessed to me that he thought he was going too far in abusing alcohol and pills, and shortly thereafter he sought residential treatment to get his addiction under control. With specialized care, he was able to return to using his own inner coping as the way to solve his problems, rather than turning to the externalizing escape of drugs.

Exercise: Identifying Your Coping Style

This exercise will help you identify whether you tend to be more of an internalizer or externalizer. If you'd like to use the checklists below to assess other people and see which coping style seems to characterize them, use the downloadable version of this exercise available at http://www .newharbinger.com/31700. (See the back of the book for instructions on how to access it. With the downloadable content, you'll also find a table summarizing these traits. You might want to print it out and keep it at hand so you can use it to quickly peg others' coping styles.)

Note that the attributes listed below lie at the extreme ends of the spectrum, accentuating the basic differences in how these two types approach life's challenges. As a reminder, in real life people are likely to exist somewhere along a continuum for these traits. Still, most people will resemble one type more than the other.

Externalizer Traits

Approach to Life

_____ Living in the present moment and not considering future consequences

_____ Thinking solutions come from the outside

_____ Looking to others to improve things: "What should someone else do to make things better?"

_____ Taking immediate action and thinking later

_____ Underestimating difficulties

Response to Problems

_____ Reacting to whatever is going on

_____ Viewing problems as someone else's fault

_____ Blaming circumstances

_____ Getting others involved in their problems

_____ Denying or escaping reality to feel better

Psychological Style

_____ Being impulsive and self-focused

_____ Believing emotions have a life of their own

_____ Getting mad easily

_____ Having no interest in the inner psychological world

Relationship Style

_____ Expecting others to provide help

_____ Thinking others should change to improve the situation

_____ Expecting others to listen and tending to engage in monologue

_____ Demanding that others stop "nagging"

Internalizer Traits

Approach to Life

_____ Worrying about the future

_____ Thinking solutions start on the inside

_____ Being thoughtful and empathic: "What can I do to make things better?"

_____ Thinking about what could happen

_____ Overestimating difficulties

Response to Problems

_____ Trying to figure out what's going on

_____ Looking for their role in causing a problem: "What's my part in this?"

_____ Engaging in self-reflection and taking responsibility

_____ Figuring out problems independently and working on them

_____ Dealing with reality as it is and being willing to change

Psychological Style

_____ Thinking before acting

_____ Believing emotions can be managed

_____ Feeling guilty easily

_____ Finding the inner psychological world fascinating

Relationship Style

_____ Thinking about what others need first

_____ Considering changing self to improve the situation

_____ Requesting dialogue about a problem

_____ Wanting to help others understand why there's a problem

If your results indicate that you're primarily an internalizer, you may feel exhausted from trying to do too much of the emotional work in your relationships. The next chapter will explore the internalizing characteristics that prompt you to do too much for others. If, on the other hand, your results indicate that you're primarily an externalizer, you might want to ask others for feedback on how you're coming across. You may be wearing out your support systems.

Balance Is the Key

People who fall at the extremes of either coping style usually have significant problems in living. Extreme externalizers tend to develop physical symptoms or get in trouble with their behavior, while extreme internalizers are prone to emotional symptoms like anxiety or depression.

If you review the checklists in the preceding exercise, you'll see that any of the traits could be a benefit or a liability depending on the circumstances. For instance, you can see that internalizers could develop self-defeating tendencies toward inaction, not speaking up, and avoiding asking for help. Conversely, although externalizers may find their life a mess, their impulsive style often makes them more willing to take action and try different solutions. Sometimes that kind of impetuousness is exactly what's needed, so in some situations it can be a strength. Under the right conditions, each style might be useful; ultimately, problems tend to arise when people get stuck at the extreme of either coping style.

Still, the overall externalizer profile does reflect a personality that's generally more unrealistic and less adaptive. This is because the extreme externalizer's immature coping mechanisms simply don't work well for successful relationships, nor do they promote mature psychological development.

Summary

Children have different ways of reacting to emotionally immature parenting, but they all develop subconscious healing fantasies about how things could get better. If a child's true self isn't accepted, the child will also adopt a role-self as a way of having a valuable part to play in the family. In addition, children develop two main coping styles in response to emotionally immature parenting: externalizing or internalizing. Externalizers think the solutions to their problems will come from outside themselves, while internalizers tend to look within themselves to solve problems. Either style might be advantageous in the moment, but internalizing is far less likely to create conflict or subject other people to hardship. Instead, the internalizer's difficulties are much more likely to result in inner distress.

In the next chapter, we'll take an in-depth look at the internalizing style. You'll see how the childhood healing fantasies of internalizers can trap them in self-defeating roles—and how recovering their true self can free them again.

Chapter 6

What It's Like to
Be an Internalizer

As children, perceptive internalizers can't help but notice it when their parents aren't truly connecting with them. They register emotional hurt in a way that a less aware child doesn't and therefore are affected deeply by growing up with emotionally immature parents. Because internalizers are sensitive to the subtleties of their relationships with loved ones, when they have an emotionally unengaged parent, they are much more aware of the painful loneliness that results.

In this chapter, we'll take a closer look at the characteristics of internalizers. We'll also explore the pitfalls of an internalizing style, particularly how hopes for a close connection can lead people to do too much for others, to the point of neglecting themselves.

Internalizers Are Highly Sensitive and Perceptive

If you're an internalizer, you may wonder how you ended up being so alert to other people's inner states. It could be that you were prompted to be so attuned to the feelings and needs of others by something as basic as your nervous system.

Internalizers are extremely sensitive and, far more than most people, notice everything. They react to life as if they were an emotional tuning fork, picking up and resonating with vibrations from other people and the world around them. This perceptiveness can be both a blessing and a curse. As one client described it to me, "My brain absorbs everything! I can't believe how much stuff I pick up on, it seeps right into me."

Internalizers may have an exceptionally alert nervous system from birth. Some research has found that differences in babies' levels of attunement to the environment can be seen at a very early age (Porges 2011). Even as five-month-old infants, some babies show more perceptiveness and sustained interest than others (Conradt, Measelle, and Ablow 2013). Further, these characteristics were found to be correlated with the kinds of behaviors children engaged in as they matured.

In his review of his own and others' research, neuroscientist Stephen Porges (2011) has made a strong case that innate neurological differences exist even in newborns. His research suggests that, from early in life, people may differ widely in their ability to self-soothe and regulate physiological functions when under stress. To me, this seems to indicate the possibility that a predisposition to a certain coping style may exist from infancy.

Internalizers Have Strong Emotions

Internalizers don't act out their emotions immediately, like externalizers do, so their feelings have a chance to intensify as they're held inside. And because they feel things deeply, it isn't surprising that internalizers are often seen as overly sensitive or too emotional. When internalizers experience a painful emotion, they're much more likely to look sad or cry—just the sort of display an emotionally phobic parent can't stand. On the other hand, when externalizers have strong feelings, they act them out in behavior before they experience much internal distress. Therefore, other people are likely to see externalizers as having a behavior problem rather than an emotional issue, even though emotions are causing the behavior.

Emotionally immature parents may yell at or punish externalizers for their behavior, whereas they're more likely to dismiss or reject internalizers' feelings with shaming, contempt, or derision. And while externalizers are told that their behavior is a problem, internalizers get the message that their very nature is the problem. For example, one woman's father sarcastically said that if she ever wrote a book about her life, she should call it *Crying Over Spilt Milk*. She was deeply hurt because she knew her emotional intensity was a characteristic she could never change. Her father's sarcasm had zeroed in on her very core.

Internalizers Have a Deep Need for Connection

Because they're so attuned to feelings, internalizers are extremely sensitive to the quality of emotional intimacy in their relationships. Their entire personality longs for emotional spontaneity and intimacy, and they can't be satisfied with less. Therefore, when they're raised by immature and emotionally phobic parents, they feel painfully lonely.

If there's anything internalizers have in common, it's their need to share their inner experience. As children, their need for genuine emotional connection is the central fact of their existence. Nothing hurts their spirit more than being around someone who won't engage with them emotionally. A blank face kills something in them. They read people closely, looking for signs that they've made a connection. This isn't a social urge, like wanting people to chat with; it's a powerful hunger to connect heart to heart with a like-minded person who can understand them. They find nothing more exhilarating than clicking with someone who gets them. When they can't make that kind of connection, they feel emotional loneliness.

From chapter 4, you may recall that this need for emotional responsiveness and reciprocal interaction from the parent is normal in securely attached babies. It's how parent-child bonding takes place. Research has demonstrated that securely attached babies demonstrate distress and break down if their mothers stop responding to them and show only an expressionless face (Tronick, Adamson, and Brazelton 1975). The poignancy of this distress can be viewed online at YouTube with the keyword search "still face experiment."

When internalizing children have self-involved parents, they often think that being helpful and hiding their needs will win their parents' love. Unfortunately, being counted on isn't the same thing as being loved, and the emotional emptiness of this strategy eventually becomes apparent. No child can be good enough to evoke love from a highly self-involved parent. Nevertheless, these children come to believe that the price of making a connection is to put other people first and treat them as more important. They think they can keep relationships by being the giver. Children who try to be good enough to win their parents' love have no way of knowing that unconditional love cannot be bought with conditional behavior.

Logan's Story

Logan, a forty-one-year-old professional musician, entered my office with a buzz of intensity, her red hair billowing like a storm cloud. She was dressed all in black and as skinny as a burnt match. She wasted no time in getting to the point.

She had come to psychotherapy because of her increasing irritability with people and an inability to unwind and relax. She knew that many of her issues were based in the anger she felt toward her family for their lack of emotional responsiveness to her. Although she came from a conventional, religious family that emphasized family closeness and loyalty, she didn't feel a connection with them. She couldn't figure out how to interact with her parents and siblings in such a way that she could have a relationship with them and still be herself.

"I get so tired of their unresponsiveness," Logan said angrily. "I can't get them to listen to me or even see me for who I am." But then her shoulders sagged, and in a small, less confident voice, she said, "I was raised to be a good little girl, but I didn't do that very well. When I got upset, they ignored me. I could be on fire and they wouldn't notice."

Underneath Logan's anger was a long-standing sadness. She'd been struggling to make sense of why she felt so rejected by her parents' seemingly normal behavior. Her feelings of isolation didn't match the official family story of loving togetherness. She wondered whether something was wrong with her; perhaps she had always been too much for them?

As an internalizer, Logan had a strong need for authentic emotional connection. Unfortunately, her self-preoccupied siblings and parents weren't interested in that kind of relationship. No one in her family paid attention to feelings, and her expressions of enthusiasm fell on deaf ears. In keeping with their emotional immaturity, her parents were intent on playing out their narrow family roles, as were her siblings.

Logan summed up by saying, "My parents are utterly unempathetic. We're never on the same wavelength. They don't want to be on my wavelength. It's safer for them, but for me it's exhausting."

Try as she might, Logan couldn't turn herself into the kind of conventional person her emotionally immature parents could relate to, and she felt defeated in her attempts to have more real closeness with them. Her failed efforts had sent her into a crisis of self-doubt and intense confusion. Was she crazy for needing so much from them?

Logan had been on fire with emotional pain for a long time, but no one had noticed because she was so smart and successful. Yet despite her accomplishments, Logan's lack of emotional closeness with her family left her feeling empty inside. To compensate for this lack of connection, Logan often tried to make people smile and feel good. She felt she would be valued only for what she could do for others, not for who she was.

Internalizers Have Strong Instincts for Genuine Engagement

Feelings of isolation and disconnection are stressful, but have you ever thought about why? Is it just less pleasant or less fun to be by yourself? Or perhaps there's something deeper going on, something so basic to humans that some of the worst punishments ever devised include shunning, ostracism, solitary confinement, and exile. Why is emotional connection so crucial?

According to neuroscientist Stephen Porges (2011), mammals have evolved a unique coping instinct in which they are calmed by proximity or engagement with others. Instead of just having the involuntary stress reactions of fight, flight, or freeze, like reptiles do, mammals can calm their heart rate and reduce the physical costs of stress by seeking reassuring contact with others of their kind. Certain vagus nerve pathways in mammals have evolved to allow stress hormones and heart rate to be reduced by comforting in such forms as physical closeness, touch, soothing sounds, and even eye contact. These calming effects conserve valuable energy and also create pleasurable social bonds that promote strong groups.

For all mammals, including humans, something magical happens when this desire to seek comfort switches on. The danger might not go away, but individuals can stay relatively calm as long as they feel tied into their herd, pack, or circle of loved ones. Most mammals have stressful lives, but thanks to their instinct for engaging with others, calming comfort and restored energy are just a friendly contact away. This gives mammals a tremendous advantage over other animals when it comes to dealing with stress in an energy-efficient way, since they don't have to go into fight, flight, or freeze every time they sense a threat.

Understanding That Connection Is Normal, Not Dependent

It's crucial that internalizers see their instinctive desire for emotional engagement as a positive thing, rather than interpreting it to mean they're too needy or dependent. Instinctively turning to others for comfort when stressed makes people stronger and more adaptive. Even if they've been shamed by an unresponsive parent for needing attention, their emotional needs show that their healthy mammalian instinct for seeking comfort is working well. Internalizers instinctively know that there's strength in being interdependent, as all mammals evolved to be. Only emotionally phobic, emotionally immature people believe that wanting empathy and understanding is a sign of weakness.

Forging Emotional Connections Outside the Family

Due to their perceptiveness and strong needs for social engagement, children who are internalizers are usually adept at finding potential sources of emotional connection outside the family. They notice when people respond to them warmly, and they naturally seek out relationships with safe people outside the family to gain an increased sense of security. Many of my clients have warm memories of a neighbor, relative, or teacher who made a huge difference in helping them feel valued and attended to. Others found similar support from pets or childhood buddies. Internalizers may even feel emotionally nurtured as they resonate with the beauty of nature or art. Spirituality can also provide this emotional nurturance, as internalizers experience and relate to a greater presence that accompanies them no matter what.

Externalizers also have needs for emotional comforting, but they tend to force such needs on other people, taking others emotionally hostage with their reactivity. They often use their behavior to coerce certain responses from other people, but because they achieve these responses through manipulation, the attention they receive is never as satisfying as a free and genuine exchange of emotional intimacy. Externalizers also demand attention by blaming or guilt-tripping others. As a result, people may end up feeling that they *have* to help, whether they want to or not, creating resentment over the long run.

The Relationship Between Avoiding Engagement and Emotional Immaturity

Most emotionally immature people tend to be externalizers who don't know how to calm themselves through genuine emotional engagement. When they feel insecure, instead of seeking comfort from other people they tend to feel threatened and launch into fight, flight, or freeze behaviors. They react to anxious moments in relationships with rigid, defensive behaviors that alienate other people, rather than bringing them closer. Anger, blame, criticism, and domination are all signs of poorly functioning skills in seeking comfort. Externalizers simply don't know how to reach out for soothing.

Externalizers who get very upset may look like they have a strong drive toward emotional engagement, but their approach is more like panicking than connecting. It takes a lot to calm them, and even then they still seem vaguely mistrustful and dissatisfied because they aren't open to connecting fully. Trying to calm an upset externalizer is an unsatisfying experience for both people, as the person providing comfort has no sense of truly helping.

The Role of Emotional Connection Skills in Physical Survival

A strong drive for comforting through close connection has benefits beyond just making people feel better. It can be a lifesaver. Using close relationships for reassurance and support is one of the traits that help people survive extreme, life-threatening conditions (Gonzales 2003). If a person's only way of coping is to fight, flee, or freeze up when things become stressful, imagine how hard it would be for that person to endure a lengthy survival challenge. Research into people who live through nearly impossible circumstances shows that they invariably call upon their present relationships and memories of loved ones as sources of inspiration and determination to survive.

Given that emotional connection is powerful enough to support people through catastrophic events, think what it can do for ordinary daily coping. Everyone needs a deep sense of connection in order to feel fully secure, and there's nothing weak about it.

Internalizers Are Apologetic About Needing Help

When internalizers finally seek help, including therapy, they often feel embarrassed and undeserving. Internalizers who grew up with emotionally immature parents are always surprised to have their feelings taken seriously. They often downplay their suffering as being over "silly things" or "stupid stuff." Some even comment that they shouldn't be taking up therapy time when there are so many other people who need help more than they do—probably indicating that they grew up in a family where attention-demanding externalizers were the only ones deemed in need of help.

If internalizers were shamed for their sensitive emotions during childhood, as adults they may be embarrassed to show any deep emotion. They may say "I'm sorry" when they start crying in a therapist's office, as though they should be able to talk about their emotional pain without showing it. Some even bring their own tissues because they don't want to use up the therapist's. They're convinced that their deepest feelings are a nuisance to other people.

Internalizers are always caught off guard when someone shows genuine interest in how they feel. One overwhelmed woman who had just started psychotherapy paused in her story and looked at me oddly. She then said in amazement, "You really *see* me." She could tell I understood the underlying pain she was describing despite her exceptionally high functioning in daily life. She acted like this was the last thing she expected, and given that she was an internalizer, it most assuredly was.

Internalizers Become Invisible and Easy to Neglect

Externalizers are the easy children to spot in a family system: a kid who blows up over nothing, a teenager who keeps getting in trouble, an adult child who causes problems. Whatever their issues, externalizers are always the ones in the foreground of their parents' concern. Their parents devote more energy and worry to them than their other kids.

Internalizers often appear to need less attention and nurturance than externalizers because they rely on their inner resources. Being internalizers, they're embarrassed to ask for help and instead try to solve problems on their own. They hate to feel like a bother. This makes them low-maintenance children who are easy to overlook. For busy or preoccupied parents, this self-reliance may invite neglect. Parents may think their child is getting by just fine without much attention. Indeed, self-contained internalizers do seem to get by on less attention; but this doesn't mean they can get by on emotional neglect.

Because emotionally immature parents see their internalizing children as better able to take care of themselves, they allow these independent children to have more of a life outside the family. But even though internalizers can cope more independently, they still long to connect with their parents and capture their interest. Being emotionally invisible is not okay for any child, especially sensitive and emotionally attuned internalizers.

Getting By on Limited Recognition

As they grow up, emotionally neglected internalizers continue to feel they should do everything on their own, and they are often quite adept at this. Because internalizers like to learn and remember experiences, they're able to store up whatever they do get from others, helping them go a long time between moments of attention and affection. Using their excellent emotional memory, they can turn within themselves when they aren't getting much nurturance from others. One of my clients called it "getting by on vapors" and explained, "Social connection is like a trace mineral or vitamin. You don't need a lot, but you can get sick if you don't have *any*."

One man was so accustomed to helping other people that he was stunned when his sister expressed her gratitude for everything he'd done over the years. Being noticed was so unexpected for him that his sister's kindness nearly bowled him over. Because internalizers routinely take on so much responsibility for others, they're deeply grateful for even the smallest bit of recognition. In fact, this is one of the hallmarks of an internalizer: an almost over-the-top gratitude for any kind of recognition or special affection.

Recognizing Childhood Neglect

Emotional immaturity in parents guarantees that their children will experience significant emotional neglect. However, this emotional deprivation is often a silent and invisible experience for children. These children will feel the emptiness but won't know what to call it. They'll grow up suffering from emotional loneliness, but won't know what's wrong. They'll just feel different from people who seem truly at ease. (If you're interested in exploring whether you may have experienced emotional deprivation in childhood, the 1993 book *Reinventing Your Life*, by Jeffrey Young and Janet Klosko, offers additional information to help people determine if they were emotionally deprived.)

People often have no idea that they've experienced emotional neglect until the first time they read about it. When these people come to psychotherapy, they typically don't identify themselves as having been neglected. But upon deeper examination, they often have memories that reveal that they didn't feel properly watched over as children. These memories often involve feeling alone and unprotected in potentially dangerous situations or feeling that parents or caregivers weren't sufficiently concerned about what might happen to them. Often, they simply knew that they needed to be vigilant, watching out for and taking care of themselves. One woman recalled that, as a four-year-old, she was left alone on a beach for over an hour without her mother trying to find her, and others corroborated this memory. Another person recalled visiting a swimming pool as a young child and staying away from the edge of the pool because she was sure her mother wasn't keeping an eye on her.

Again, the self-sufficiency of internalizing children tends to create the impression that they have no needs. They're expected to be okay and get along without anyone watching over them carefully. They may be characterized as "old souls," with their parents counting on them to do the right thing. They willingly oblige, playing a role that's overly self-reliant, which often leads to an adult life of overextending themselves for others.

———Sandra's Story———

When Sandra was eleven, she and her seven-year-old brother were sent to another state to stay with relatives for the summer. With apparently no concern, their mother put them on a bus for five-hundred-mile overnight journey in which they had to change buses in the middle of the night. Although Sandra felt lost and afraid, she knew she had to protect her little brother. Situations that might make another child panic send internalizers into an intensely focused state while they figure out how to take care of things. As Sandra put it, "My brother was really scared and cried a lot. I was stoic. I knew it was up to me to make the best of it."

Bethany's Story

Bethany was sent to Brazil one summer as a ten-year-old to be a babysitter for the infant son of her irresponsible older brother and his new young wife. The brother and sister-in-law liked to party and came and went as they pleased while ten-year-old Bethany took care of her baby nephew. When the summer ended, her mother had Bethany stay in Brazil and miss school so that she could keep helping her brother's family. Finally, something seemed to stir in her mother back home, and she went and retrieved Bethany. Her mother was a classic example of a self-preoccupied, emotionally immature parent: blind to the fact that the capable internalizer is still a child and needs to be looked out for.

Learning to Ignore One's Own Feelings

Children who had to become tough and handle things on their own may develop a rejecting attitude toward their own feelings. Perhaps they learned to keep distance from painful feelings they knew their emotionally immature parent couldn't help them with.

Leah's Story

One day in therapy, Leah, who had grown up in an atmosphere of emotional neglect, apologized to me for "still being depressed." She was convinced that I found her sadness annoying and exasperating.

Leah thought the only thing I wanted to hear was that she was all better so that I could feel good about myself as a successful therapist. It was hard for her to imagine I could be interested in how she was really feeling. This was a remnant of her childhood, when her emotionally cold and critical mother became clearly irritated anytime Leah expressed her emotions. In response, Leah developed the belief that the best way to connect was to become a "likable" person with no emotional needs. So she hid her feelings and tried to play a role others would like.

Throughout her childhood, Leah tried to be self-sufficient. She often wondered, *How can I make myself enough? How can I feel secure?* It didn't occur to her that these weren't questions for a child to answer. Only an emotionally attentive parent could have made her feel that being herself was enough.

Receiving Only Superficial Support

Another form of neglect occurs when emotionally immature parents give such superficial comfort that they aren't at all helpful to a scared child. One woman remembered that whenever she was scared as a child, she knew she would have to get through it on her own. When I asked whether she remembered ever getting help with her fears, she said, "That feels like a foreign idea to me. It would be nice to know someone understands, but I never felt that way. I don't remember anyone being able to help with the fears I was having. They just said generic things, like 'Oh, you're going to be fine,' 'It's going to be okay,' or 'There's no need to feel that way; you'll feel better soon.'"

Internalizers Are Overly Independent

Emotional neglect can make premature independence feel like a virtue. Many people who were neglected as children don't realize that their independence was a necessity, not a choice. I've had clients describe this to me in a number of ways, such as "I've always been the one looking out for myself," "It's nothing I can't handle myself; I don't like to rely on anyone," and "You should be able to do it without anyone else. Don't let them see you sweat."

Unfortunately, children who become so independent may not learn how to ask for help later in life when it's readily available. It often falls to psychotherapists or other counselors to coax these people into accepting their need for help as legitimate.

Internalizers Don't See Abuse for What It Is

Because internalizers look within themselves for reasons why things go wrong, they may not always recognize abuse for what it is. If parents don't label their own behavior as abusive, their child won't label it that way either. Even as adults, many people have no idea that what happened to them in childhood was abusive. As a result, they may not recognize abusive behavior in their adult relationships.

For instance, Vivian hesitated to tell me about her husband's anger, saying it was too silly and insignificant to talk about. She then sheepishly told me that he'd broken things when angry and once threw her craft project on the floor because he wanted her to keep the house neater. As it turned out, Vivian was embarrassed to tell me because she thought I'd say his behavior was normal and tell her she was making a mountain out of a molehill.

Another client, a middle-aged man, recounted incidents of childhood abuse nonchalantly, with no recognition of how serious it had been. For example, he said his father once choked him until he wet himself and then locked him in the basement. Recalling that his father had once thrown a stereo set, he admitted that his father "might have had a temper." As he spoke, his demeanor clearly indicated that he accepted this behavior as normal.

Internalizers Do Most of the Emotional Work in Relationships

Internalizers put a lot of emotional work into their family relationships. As a reminder, emotional work involves using empathy, foresight, and self-control to foster relationships and get along well with others. In healthy families, parents do most of the emotional work with their children. But when parents aren't coping well, an internalizing child often steps into the parenting gap. This may take the form of being overly responsible, such as caring for younger siblings when parents are swamped with a crisis, or it could mean paying attention to everyone's feelings to see who's upset and needs to be calmed down.

Adopting Compensatory Cheerfulness

Especially when their parents are depressed or emotionally flat, internalizing children may take on a cheerful, lighthearted role, trying to bring happiness and liveliness into an otherwise somber family climate. With their liveliness and good sense of humor, they help others feel that things aren't so bad. One woman described playing such a role this way: "I was always the happy one. For example, during the holidays I'd be the one saying, 'Let's put the decorations up!' I did it because people in my family were so detached and unenthusiastic. I now realize I was looking for a connection." She was doing a lot of emotional work to get her family to be excited with her, even if it meant she had to single-handedly inject them with the holiday spirit.

Doing Emotional Work for Parents

Emotionally immature parents avoid emotional work if they can. As a result, they may not deal with their children's emotional or attention problems or difficulties at school, leaving the children to flounder on their own. When their children need emotional support, these parents are especially unhelpful. For example, they may be dismissive when their child feels hurt or rejected by peers. Instead of trying to understand their child's social predicament, they toss out useless or flippant advice. Ultimately, children learn that these parents simply won't do any emotional work to help them with their hurt feelings.

Furthermore, internalizers' natural sensitivity prompts them to do emotional work for their parents. Sometimes the internalizing child's emotional work even extends to parenting the parent—listening to them, offering reassurance, and even giving advice. These children can get roped into playing the role of emotional support person long before they're mature enough to do so. Worse, sometimes a parent dumps painful emotional issues on a child but then brushes off any advice the child tries to give—a role-reversal that can continue long into adulthood. In addition to being a no-win situation, this demands excessive emotional work from the child.

——Candace's Story——

From childhood and into adulthood, Candace had provided a listening ear for her mother's chronic relationship problems. When I asked how she came to play this frustrating role with her mother, Candace said, "I know I'm more emotionally stable than she is. I'm used to handling my own issues without my mother's help. She's definitely the neediest one in our relationship. She needs my encouragement to stand up for herself. She's always had an issue about feeling unlovable. Her self-esteem isn't there. I'm just trying to help her find happiness."

Overworking in Adult Relationships

Many internalizing children optimistically believe that when they grow up, they'll be able to single-handedly love another person into a good relationship. Reflecting on her failing marriage, one woman put it this way: "I thought I could be enough for both of us." Internalizers are accustomed to supplying most of the empathy and doing more than their fair share in trying to get along, and for a long time they may not notice that they're getting worn out while the other person isn't changing at all.

Internalizers sometimes take up emotional slack by playing *both parts* in their interactions with people. They act as if there's reciprocity when there isn't. For instance, they might thank someone for being patient when they are actually the ones being inconvenienced, or they might repeatedly reach out to self-centered people with a thoughtfulness they never get back. They are so familiar with supplying the sensitivity that was missing in their family members that they automatically do this with everyone. They make up for other people's lack of engagement by seeing them as nicer and more considerate than they really are.

One man told me about an optimistic fantasy he had regarding his girlfriend, saying, "I thought I could somehow be so wonderful that she would feel something for me that doesn't come to her naturally. I was sure I could make her happy and make her love me." He'd believed that his girlfriend's feelings were something he could change.

A female client revealed how much extra emotional work she did in all her friendships, "My problem is that I always try to be nice and accommodating. If I think about what I want or need, I worry that others will think I'm uncaring or trying to be mean. I feel like I have to be concerned about them all the time or I'm a bad person."

Another woman only realized after her divorce how much emotional work she'd been doing in the relationship: "When my husband would get worked up over small things, instead of telling him, 'That's completely ridiculous,' I tried to calm and accommodate him. He was so emotionally inept. How did I miss that for ten years? I didn't see how much effort I was putting in. Instead, I told myself, *We are both trying to make this work.* I thought maybe I wasn't a good enough wife and wondered what I could do differently—what I could do to improve things. I figured that everyone struggles, and maybe this was just what marriage is like."

Why do internalizers so often end up in lopsided relationships where they do more than their fair share of the emotional work? One reason is that needy externalizers tend to pursue warm and giving internalizers. Initially, they make the internalizer feel special in order to secure the relationship, but once they have the person, they stop doing the emotional work of reciprocating. The internalizers are surprised at this turnaround, and often blame themselves.

Attracting Needy People

From an early age, internalizers can seem so self-contained that emotionally immature people can't resist leaning on them. Internalizers are so perceptive and sensible that even people they've never met before may instinctively trust them in a stressful situation. My client Martine described it this way: "I'm the go-to person for support and an ear—the voice of calm and wisdom. People don't get that kind of response much, so they flock to me like I'm a dumping ground for their problems. I'm just trying to be a good friend and supportive person, but it encourages people to put too much of their stuff on me. This is something that happens to me a lot."

Without even knowing it, people like Martine exude an aura of kindliness and wisdom that's powerfully attractive to needy people. Fortunately, Martine eventually did realize that, for her own good, she needed to be more selective about extending her natural empathy and altruism. As she stopped giving her time and attention indiscriminately, she gained more energy for her own life.

In the course of therapy, another client finally realized how widespread her automatic caretaking had become, extending even to people she didn't know. She found herself engaging with chatty strangers in elevators and lonely passersby who tried to strike up unwanted conversations. *Do I have a sign around my neck?* she wondered. She felt obligated to give everyone a warm response, doing emotional work even for people she'd never seen before. And the fact is, needy strangers will gobble up a sensitive person's attention if given half a chance, whether on an airplane, in an elevator, or while waiting in line.

Believing That Self-Neglect Will Bring Love

Many internalizers subconsciously believe that neglecting oneself is a sign of being a good person. When self-absorbed parents make excessive claims on their children's energy and attention, they teach them that self-sacrifice is the worthiest ideal—a message that internalizing children are likely to take very seriously. These children don't realize that their self-sacrifice has been pushed to unhealthy levels due to their parents' self-centeredness. Sometimes these parents use religious principles to promote self-sacrifice, making their children feel guilty for wanting anything for themselves. In this way, religious ideas that should be spiritually nourishing are instead used to keep idealistic children focused on taking care of others.

Children don't inherently know how to protect their energies. They must be taught how to engage in good self-care—something that happens when adults pay attention to their needs and reinforce the fact that they need rest, sympathy, and respect. For example, sensitive parents teach their children to notice and identify their fatigue, instead of making them feel anxious and lazy for needing to rest.

Unfortunately, emotionally immature parents are so self-focused that they don't notice when their children are getting overwhelmed or trying too hard. They're more likely to take advantage of a child's sensitive, caring nature, rather than protect the child from overusing it. And if parents don't teach their children about good self-care, in adulthood those children won't know how to keep a healthy emotional balance between their needs and the needs of others.

This is especially the case with internalizers. Because of their attunement to others, they can get so focused on other people's issues that they lose sight of their own needs and overlook how the emotional drain is harming them. In addition, they are secretly convinced that more self-sacrifice and emotional work will eventually transform their unsatisfying relationships. So the greater the difficulties, the more they try.

If this seems illogical, remember that these healing fantasies are based on a *child's* ideas about how to make things better. As children, internalizers tend to take on the role-self of the rescuer, feeling a responsibility to help others even to the point of self-neglect. Their healing fantasy always involves the idea *It's up to me to fix this.* What they can't see is that they've taken on a job nobody has ever pulled off: changing people who aren't seeking to change themselves.

It's hard for internalizers to give up the fight to be loved, but sometimes they eventually realize that they can't single-handedly change how another person relates to them. They finally feel resentment and begin to withdraw emotionally. When an internalizer ultimately does give up, the other person may be caught off guard, since the internalizer had continued to reach out and try to connect for so long.

Summary

Internalizers are highly perceptive and extremely sensitive to other people. Because of their strong need to connect, growing up with an emotionally immature parent is especially painful for them. Internalizers have strong emotions but shrink from bothering other people, making them easy for emotionally immature parents to neglect. They develop a role-self that's overly focused on other people, along with a healing fantasy that they can change others' feelings and behaviors toward them. They get by on very little support from others and end up doing too much emotional work in their relationships, which can lead to resentment and exhaustion.

In the next chapter, we'll take a look at what happens when internalizers' true self finally wakes up and they see that they've been giving too much.

Chapter 7

Breaking Down
and Awakening

This chapter describes what it's like for people to wake up from an ill-fitting role they've been playing for too long. This awakening stage often starts with a sense of failure or loss of control. Painful symptoms like depression, anxiety, chronic tension, or not sleeping can all be signals that old strategies to rewrite reality have become unsustainable. These psychological and physical symptoms are a warning system, telling us that we need to get back in sync with who we are and how we really feel.

What Is the True Self?

The concept of the true self goes all the way back to ancient times when the idea of having a soul first arose. Human beings have always felt the presence of a genuine inner self that sees and experiences everything but stands a little apart from what we do in the outside world. This self is the source of our unique individuality and is unaffected by the family pressures that mold our role-selves. This inner self has been known by many names—such as the true self, the real self, the core self (Fosha 2000)—but all are the same thing: the consciousness that speaks the truth at the center of a person's being.

You can think of the true self as an extremely accurate, self-informing neurological feedback system that points each individual toward optimal energy and functioning. The physical sensations that accompany experiencing the true self suggest that whatever this self is, it's based in our biology as human beings. It's the source of all gut feelings and intuition, including immediate, accurate impressions of other people. We can use fluctuations in the energy of our true selves as a guidance system to tell us when we're in alignment with a life path that fits us well (Gibson 2000).

When we're in accord with our true selves, we see things clearly and feel that we're in a state of flow. We become focused on solutions instead of problems. Things seem much more possible as we pay attention to our genuine needs and desires. Opportunities and people come into our lives that help us in ways we never imagined. We actually become "luckier."

What Does the True Self Want?

Your true self has the same needs as a flourishing, healthy child: to grow, be known, and express itself. Above all, your true self keeps pushing for your expansion, as if your self-actualization were the most important thing on earth. To this end, it asks for your acceptance of its guidance and legitimate desires. It has no interest in whatever desperate ideas you came up with in childhood regarding a healing fantasy or role-self. It only wants to be genuine with other people and sincere in its own pursuits.

Children stay in alignment with their true self if the important adults in their lives support doing so. However, when they're criticized or shamed, they learn to feel embarrassed by their true desires. By pretending to be what their parents want, children think they've found the way to win their parents' love. They silence their true selves and instead follow the guidance of their role-selves and fantasies. In the process, they lose touch with both their inner and outer reality.

Exercise: Awakening to Your True Self

Whether you're an internalizer or an externalizer, if you've been asleep to your deepest needs, your true self will use emotional symptoms to wake you up so you can start taking care of yourself. Your true self wants you to have the peace of living in accordance with reality. The trick is to recognize these signs of distress for the lifesavers they are.

This exercise will help you become more conscious of your true self. You'll need a single piece of paper and a pen. Fold the piece of paper lengthwise down the middle, so you can only see one half of the page at a time, then write a heading on each half: "My True Self" and My Role-Self."

First, orient the paper so you only see the half with the heading "My True Self." Then think back to yourself as a child. Go deep and be honest. What were you like before you started trying to be someone else? Before you learned to judge and criticize yourself, what did you enjoy doing? What made you feel good? If you could be the person you really are (and didn't have to worry about money), what would your life be like right now?

I recommend looking back to who you were before fourth grade. What were you interested in? Who were your favorite people, and what did you like about them? If you had free time, what did you like to do? How did you like to play? What was your idea of a perfect day? What really raised your energies? Write down your thoughts about this in no particular order, as they come to you, beneath the heading "My True Self."

When you finish that list, flip the paper over to the half with the heading "My Role-Self." Contemplate who you've had to become in order to feel admired and loved. Are you now involved in things that you aren't really interested in? What do you make yourself do because you think it means you're a good person? Are there people you are involved with who deplete your energy and make you feel drained? What are you spending time on that's boring to you? How would you describe the social role you try to play? How do you hope others see you? Which of your personality traits do you try to cover up? What are you glad nobody knows about you?

When you finish, put the piece of paper away for at least a day. Then open it up, smooth it down the middle, and compare the two sides. Are you primarily living from your true self, or is your role-self dominating your life?

Breaking Down in Order to Wake Up

People experience a breakdown when the pain of living in role-selves and healing fantasies begins to outweigh any potential benefits. Most psychological growth exposes some distressing truths about what we've been doing with our lives. Psychotherapy and the like are aids to help us become aware of truths we already know in our bones. When you're going through a breakdown, a good question to ask is what is actually breaking down. We usually think it's our self. But what's typically happening is that our struggle to deny our emotional truth is breaking down. Emotional distress is a signal that it's getting harder to remain emotionally unconscious. It means we're about to discover our true selves underneath all that story business.

Your true self wants you to see what's really going on. It tries to wake you up because it wants you to stop believing that your emotionally immature parents knew what was best for you and that creating a role-self is better than being who you really are. It knows better than to let a fantasy run your life.

Developmental psychologist Jean Piaget (1963) observed that in order for people to learn anything new, their old mental pattern must break up and rework itself around the new, incoming knowledge. This process of internal breakdown and accommodation is key to continuing intellectual development. Likewise, Polish psychiatrist Kazimierz Dabrowski (1972) theorized that emotional distress is potentially a sign of growth, not necessarily illness. He saw psychological symptoms as coming from a freshly activated urge to grow and coined the term "positive disintegration" to describe times when people break down inside in order to reorganize into more emotionally complex beings.

Dabrowski noticed that some people were able to expand their personalities as a result of these upheavals, while others soon slipped back to where they'd been before. He observed that psychologically unaware people weren't likely to change much after an emotional upheaval. Other people, however, seemed to take periods of distress as opportunities to learn about themselves, meeting challenging emotional conditions with curiosity and a desire to learn from them. Dabrowski felt that these people had a developmental potential that pushed them toward becoming more competent and autonomous.

Dabrowski believed that individuals who can tolerate negative emotions tend to have the highest developmental potential and saw negative emotions as the driving force behind much of human psychological development, since the discomfort these feelings cause can motivate ambitious people to find solutions. Instead of shutting down or getting defensive when faced with difficult experiences, people with developmental potential try to discover a deeper understanding about themselves and reality. To this end, they're willing to engage in self-reflection, even if this entails painful self-doubt. Although the uncertainty inherent in this process of self-examination can create the by-products of anxiety, guilt, or depression, tackling these deep questions ultimately yields a stronger, more adaptive personality.

Aileen's Story

My client Aileen found support and validation in Dabrowski's ideas. An insightful woman, she had benefited greatly from psychotherapy over the years. Her love of learning made her want to understand herself and other people, but her family saw that kind of psychological interest as a sign of maladjustment.

When Aileen sought therapy after a very destructive love affair, her family thought she was being ridiculous and labeled her "the sick one." Rather than seeing that Aileen was using her emotional pain as a tool for growth and self-understanding, they wondered why she was wasting so much time and money rehashing the past.

Aileen knew she was doing the right thing by coming to therapy but worried that maybe she *was* the sick one in the family. At one level she knew better, based on her awareness of her parents' immaturity, impulsivity, and avoidance of emotional intimacy. But it still seemed odd to her that she was the only family member who felt the need for help.

Learning about Dabrowski's idea of positive disintegration helped Aileen see her distress as growing pains. And once she knew about Dabrowski's growth theory, she felt proud of herself for being the only person in her family willing to explore her distress in order to find a healthier way of being.

Waking Up from an Outdated Role-Self

People often keep playing their childhood role-self far into adulthood because they believe it keeps them safe and is the only way to be accepted. But when the true self has had enough of the role-playing, people often get a wake-up call in the form of unexpected emotional symptoms.

——Virginia's Story——

Virginia's wake-up call came in the form of sudden onset of panic attacks that occurred when she felt criticized by her tyrannical and judgmental older brother, Brian. Virginia had always worried constantly about what people thought of her, so much so that social events were exhausting triathlons of reading other people, trying not to give offense, and imagining imminent rejection. At work, she miserably obsessed over how people saw her. Virginia came to therapy to get a grip on her panic (and did), but she also ended up realizing how unaccepted she'd felt as a child.

Through therapy, Virginia realized that Brian had the same disapproving manner as their deceased father, who had always left Virginia feeling inept and unloved. She began to understand that her social anxiety was a reflection of her childhood role, in which she repeatedly and unsuccessfully tried to win the love of her critical and disdainful father. Her subconscious healing fantasy was that one day she would finally be "correct" enough to gain his approval. She had unconsciously taken on the role of playing the scared, inadequate child to her father's wise and powerful persona, and now Brian was his stand-in.

Virginia's anxiety attacks signaled that she was beginning to question her childhood belief that the authority figure is always right. She told me, "If people expressed any displeasure with me, especially men, I got frightened and automatically assumed I must be wrong." But now she was able to see her relationship with Brian more clearly: "I've been putting him on a pedestal, like he's some kind of god. He doesn't care about me, yet I let him determine whether I felt good or not. I've always been so concerned about his opinion, but now I'm getting a bit more self-contained. I feel as if I'm just learning to be an individual."

Without the wake-up call of her panic attacks, Virginia might have just kept on deferring to others in a cloud of self-deprecating anxiety. Her panic attacks ushered in a new consciousness in which she no longer needed to accept the story of male infallibility she'd been indoctrinated with as a child—a story that had been destroying her self-esteem as an adult woman. Her role-self of being the weak and confused little girl collapsed as she realized that she could choose whether she wanted contact with Brian or not. She could finally be aware of how she really felt about her father and brother, who jointly had made her the least important member of the family. The spell was broken.

Exercise: Releasing Yourself from a Self-Defeating Role

Take a moment now to write a short personality description of someone in your life who makes you feel nervous or small. Next, think about how you behave around that person, and then write a short description of the role-self you've been playing with the person. See if you can spot a healing fantasy that might be driving you to seek this person's acceptance at all costs. How much time have you spent wishing this person would act differently toward you? Do you think you might be playing out a self-effacing role that no longer serves you? Are you ready to see yourself differently and relate to this person as you would to anyone else?

Waking Up to What You Really Feel

Sometimes giving up a healing fantasy of how we will finally win love means we have to face unwanted feelings about people close to us. Many of us tend to feel guilty and ashamed for feelings we deem to be unacceptable. We're convinced that the only way to be a good person is to repress these feelings. However, if we quash our real feelings for too long, they may bubble up in ways that force us to stop and look at what's wrong.

Tilde's Story

Tilde had so much to feel grateful for that she couldn't stop feeling guilty. She'd been born to a single mother who did domestic work to support them both. Her mother, Kajsa, had come to the United States from Sweden to make a better life for her child. She scraped together every cent she could earn so that Tilde could get a good education. Tilde had taken full advantage of her opportunities and eventually earned an advanced degree in graphic design on a scholarship. She was nearing the end of her training when she came to see me for an episode of major depression. Although she was still able to work, every morning began with a struggle to take action. As soon as she got out of bed, she longed to crawl back under the covers.

We traced the onset of her depression to phone calls to her mother, who was becoming increasingly petulant and bitter as Tilde neared completion of her studies. Kajsa had always been emotional and never let Tilde forget how she single-handedly raised her after being abandoned by Tilde's father and coming to the United States. In every conversation, Kajsa complained about physical ailments and people who had recently done her wrong. Tilde was sympathetic, and besides, she felt she owed her mother everything, but the strain of listening helplessly to Kajsa's angry misery was wearing her down. Tilde felt that nothing she said to her mother ever seemed to help.

I asked Tilde how she felt when Kajsa brushed off her sympathy and continued with her complaints. At first, Tilde would only say how guilty she felt for not being able to make her mother feel better and what a bad daughter she was for enjoying her life while Kajsa suffered. But when I persisted and asked how it felt in her body when she heard her mother's voice, Tilde finally let herself feel it. She looked stunned as she identified the feeling: "I don't like her," she said in a whisper.

This was Tilde's emotional truth, which had been at war with her childhood healing fantasy of finally giving Kajsa enough love to make up for her disappointing life. Tilde's exaggerated guilt and gratitude had prevented her from experiencing her true emotions about her mother. The ironclad family story was that Kajsa had sacrificed everything and therefore deserved Tilde's total attention and devotion. When Tilde began to resent her mother's ceaseless complaining, her guilt turned her own unacknowledged anger into depression.

Tilde's depression lifted as soon as she accepted her genuine feelings toward Kajsa. Finally allowing herself to know that she didn't like her mother, even though she was grateful to her, released her from an impossible bind. She realized that she could still have contact with her mother, but that she didn't have to pretend to feel the "right" way.

Exercise: Exploring Whether You Have Hidden Feelings

You can do this exercise anytime you're feeling especially anxious or in a down mood. At those times, ask yourself whether you might be harboring some hidden feelings. Consider the times when you feel worst and see if they're related to thinking about a certain person. (In my experience, the two feelings people seem most reluctant to admit are being afraid of someone or not liking someone.)

As you think how to put your suppressed feelings about this person into words, I recommend speaking as a fourth-grader might, using simple, clear sentences. Also, work on this in a private place so you don't have to worry about other people's reactions. Then let yourself speak (or whisper) your honest truth out loud. You might try a phrase like "I don't like it when this person _____," describing their behavior. When you hit upon your true feelings, you'll feel a release of tension or sense of relief in your body. Don't let guilt inhibit you. You're speaking only to yourself, for the purpose of self-discovery. No one can hear you, and it's completely safe.

Some people think it's necessary to confront the other person to get a true resolution, but I believe this is often counterproductive and provokes too much anxiety. Disclosing feelings too soon may flood you with unnecessary anxiety—not to mention risking a backlash—when you're just beginning to get in touch with your true feelings. You can always talk to the person later if you wish, but first you need to regain your ability to speak your feelings to yourself. Just to be clear, what helps isn't telling the other person; it's knowing what you really feel. Simply admitting your true feelings and stating them out loud can make a huge difference in regaining your emotional peace.

Waking Up to Anger

Because anger is an expression of individuality, it's the emotion that emotionally immature parents most often punish their children for having. But anger can be a helpful emotion because it gives people energy to do things differently and lets them see themselves as worthy of sticking up for. It's often a good sign when overly responsible, anxious, or depressed people begin to be consciously aware of feeling angry. It indicates that their true self is coming to the fore and that they're beginning to care about themselves.

———Jade's Story———

Jade used to feel bad about herself for feeling angry so often, especially because her anger was often directed toward her parents. For years she'd thought the answer was to pretend not to have those feelings. Secretly, Jade worried that she was a malcontent who got irritated for no good reason.

But Jade's anger seemed to have its roots in how her dismissive and emotionally unengaged parents ignored her feelings. When Jade finally started thinking about her anger in terms of her emotional needs being neglected, she was able to see it differently: "Now I think there would be something wrong with me if I weren't angry! There are plenty of reasons why I'm angry, and my anger is coming right from my core self. It's very empowering to be angry. I don't want to live a lie anymore. It's been lonely and disappointing trying to relate to my parents. Being with them is isolating."

After accepting her anger, Jade could see her healing fantasy clearly for the first time. She had thought she could heal her family by being extremely loving. Here's how she put it: "I tried to see everybody as good. I thought everyone loved one another. I was naive. I thought that if you were nice to people, at the end of the day things would get fixed. I thought that my parents would actually love me, and that my brother and sister might care about what I'm interested in. But now I've learned that I need to do what's right for me and trust myself. I really do enjoy my own company. I don't want to waste my time anymore. I hope I'll find people I can trust. I'm not going to try to make it work with people who are distant or unsupportive. I'll be cordial and polite, but I'm not moving in close just to be disappointed."

Waking Up to Better Self-Care

Internalizers are notorious for not taking good care of themselves. Believing it's up to them to improve or fix everything, they often end up neglecting their own health, especially the need for rest. As they work to attend to everything they think they need to do, they often overlook even basic physical cues, including pain and fatigue.

Lena's Story

Lena lived a very pressured life in spite of her best efforts to keep things simple. She always felt like she was running out of time. It was as though there was a voice in her head that constantly told her to keep pushing herself and that her efforts were never adequate. Even pleasurable activities like playing the piano became marathons in which she had to overcome laziness and do her best. She never gave herself a break until she was completely spent.

In addition to working feverishly at her full-time job, her life was dictated by the demands she constantly perceived from others, down to her pets and the birds she fed in her yard. A drooping plant could fill her with guilt for not watering it sooner.

When Lena took an exercise class to help her relax, she wore herself out trying to keep up and do everything perfectly. During the class, she told herself, "I should be able to do this. This is baby stuff." The next morning she woke up unable to think or function very well but didn't realize she had overdone it until she tried to go up some steps, at which point she found that she was so sore she could hardly lift her legs.

Lena had a long-standing habit, promoted by her demanding mother, of ignoring her body's cues about fatigue. As a child, if she didn't get things done quickly enough or work hard enough, her mother chastised her for being lazy. As a result, she had never done things at her own pace and was insensitive to her physical limits.

Lena had been trained to believe that being a good person meant straining to achieve, even if that meant always being a little off balance and never quite ready. In Lena's quest for her mother's approval and love, she had developed the belief that she was only worth something when she was trying really hard. Her childhood healing fantasy was that one day she would try so hard that her mother would be transformed from a perennially dissatisfied taskmaster into an appreciative parent who recognized how hard her daughter was working to please her.

Lena's all-out efforts were also encouraged by society in general, through cultural maxims like "Try your hardest," "Never give up," or "Always do your best." For an overly motivated person like Lena, such messages are mind poison. It's unnecessarily exhausting to always try your best. It's more sensible to know when to do your very best and when not to. Fortunately, once Lena realized what her healing fantasy was doing to her, she was able to reset her values and take her own needs into account.

Waking Up Through Relationship Breakdowns

Relationship problems present a huge opportunity to wake up. Given that we tend to play out painful patterns learned in childhood in our significant adult relationships, it isn't surprising that so many people come for therapy because of relationship issues. And because intimate adult relationships are so emotionally arousing, they tend to activate unresolved issues about not getting our emotional needs met. We often project issues about our parents onto our partners; then we may become even more angry with them because, at an unconscious level, they remind us of the past, in addition to whatever is happening in the present.

————Mike's Story————

Mike had recently hit rock bottom after cutbacks in his work hours and a divorce that left him nearly penniless. His life had been entirely about being a success in the eyes of other people, especially his wife and his mother. Now, in therapy, he was working hard to identify values more in keeping with his true self. In the process, he was beginning to appreciate himself for who he was, including his unique strengths and talents.

As Mike reflected on his past, he said, "I didn't make decisions based on how I felt; I made decisions based on what other people wanted. I've been doing this for thirty-five years, including enduring a loveless marriage, and I have nothing to show for it. But maybe I *wanted* my recent problems to happen. Maybe I was hoping things would crumble. I've been beaten up, torn down, and humiliated, and now I'm about to be laid off, but I'm telling you, I'm *happy*."

In spite of his material losses and disappointments, Mike could finally drop the healing fantasy that he would be loved if he took care of everybody else at his own expense. The enormous financial debt he incurred due to his divorce was a fitting metaphor for what it had cost him to be someone he wasn't for so many years.

Realizing how desperate he had been to be accepted by others, Mike said, "I didn't think I was as good as other people." Then he looked at me, smiled, and asked, "So how to define a successful person?" Answering his own question, he said, "I guess, first of all, you get rid of 'success'—and then you see who you are as a person."

Waking Up from Idealizing Others

One of the hardest fantasies to wake up from is the belief that our parents are wiser and know more than we do. It can be embarrassing and even scary for children to see their parents' weaknesses. And even as adults, people may strongly resist seeing their parents' immaturity for what it is. It can feel better to remain naive about their limitations than to look at them objectively. Subconsciously, perhaps we feel protective of our parents' vulnerability.

————Patsy's Story————

My client Patsy was clearly more emotionally mature than either her impulsive husband or her petulant mother, who lived with her. However, Patsy recoiled when I observed that she seemed to be the most mature person in her family. "Oh, I don't like to think that!" she objected. She said such a thought felt disloyal and that she didn't think of herself as special or superior in any way.

Although humility can be a nice quality, it wasn't doing Patsy any good, because she was using it to ignore a glaring reality. Idealizing her mother and husband wasn't helping her; nor was denying her own strengths. Once Patsy was able to accept that she had more maturity than her husband or mother, she could be more objective about their behavior. She stopped attributing positive qualities to them that they didn't have and was able to set limits with them. She also stopped wasting energy pretending she was less than she was so that they could pretend to be more than they were.

Waking Up to Your Strengths

It's important for people to consciously appreciate their strengths. Unfortunately, the children of emotionally immature parents usually don't develop much appreciation for their positive qualities because self-involved parents have little or no ability to reflect their children's strengths. As a result, these children often feel a little embarrassed to think of themselves in terms of their most positive qualities. They're accustomed to putting others in the limelight and worry that they'll get a swelled head if they recognize their own strengths.

However, it's crucial to know what your assets are and be able to artic-ulate them. It provides self-validation and allows you to feel good about what you bring to the world. This self-recognition builds energy and posi-tivity. While modesty and humility can help you keep things in perspec-tive, they shouldn't prevent you from knowing your best qualities.

Waking Up to a New Set of Values

Family therapist and social worker Michael White developed a form of psychotherapy known as narrative therapy (2007). His approach was founded on the idea that it's crucial for people to become conscious of the meaning and intentions in the storylines they've been living by. In the process of uncovering a client's life story, the therapist works to expose the often self-neglectful values people have been living by and then invites them to update their guiding principles, choosing new values more consciously.

——————Aaron's Story——————

Aaron was a strong, silent type who had always lived by a code that involved not pushing for recognition. Growing up, he loved theater and acting, but he never spoke up to request a role or ask a director for a bigger part. He thought he would seem spoiled and demanding if he promoted himself, and that lobbying for himself was a sign of weakness.

However, as an adult, Aaron began to see that his code of not speaking up for himself often resulted in other people being put ahead of him. In addition, others often took advantage of his talents without reciprocating. He saw that his healing fantasy, in which he hoped authority figures would spontaneously recognize his potential, wasn't coming to fruition. So he decided to develop a new value of going after what he wanted. He started actively seeking opportunities and laying claim to them. Considering a job change, he said, "In the past, I would have been reluctant to do this for myself, but now I'm not." He finally saw himself as worthy of standing up for and investing in.

Waking Up by Getting Free of Childhood Issues

Working through childhood emotional injuries is the most effective way of waking up from repeating the past. When I say "working through," I mean the mental and emotional process of coming to grips with painful realities. Think of it as a process of breaking down something that's initially too big to swallow: you chew on it until it can become a digestible part of your history.

Research suggests that what has happened to people matters less than whether they've processed what happened to them. In a study of the characteristics of parents who raise securely attached children, researchers found that parents who created a secure attachment for their children were often characterized by a willingness to recall and talk about their own childhoods (Main, Kaplan, and Cassidy 1985). Even though some of these parents had lived through very difficult childhood experiences, their relationships with their own children were secure, since they had spent time thinking about and integrating their childhood experiences and were at ease with both the negative and positive aspects of their past.

It's easy to imagine why children with such parents showed secure attachment. These parents were not avoiding reality. Because they had addressed their own pasts, they were fully available to connect with their children and form a secure attachment.

Summary

The true self will find ways to express itself, even in the face of efforts to play a role or live out a healing fantasy. When people have ignored their true self for too long, they may develop psychological symptoms. Waking up to the needs of the true self can initially feel like breaking down. Panic, anger, and depression are just a few symptoms that may signal an emotional awakening to better self-care and healthier values. When people process their childhood issues and wake up to their strengths, they gain the confidence to start living from their true self.

In the next chapter, we'll explore how you can use this new objectivity and self-awareness to interact with emotionally immature family members in a new way.

Chapter 8

How to Avoid Getting Hooked by an Emotionally Immature Parent

It's hard to see our parents as fallible human beings. As children, we believe our parents can do anything. Although adolescence and the independence of adulthood can weaken our view of our parents as all-powerful, they don't eradicate it. Therefore, even if they aren't loving, we wishfully think they could be if they wanted to.

Certain cultural tenets also keep us from seeing our parents clearly. Most of us are instilled with beliefs such as these:

- All parents love their children.

- A parent is the one person you can trust.

- A parent will always be there for you.

- You can tell your parents anything.

- Your parents will love you no matter what.

- You can always go back home.

- Your parents only want what's best for you.

- Your parents know more than you do.

- Whatever your parents do, they're doing it for your own good.

But if your parents were emotionally immature, many of these statements may not be true.

In this chapter, I'll help you look beneath the surface of your childhood hopes and cultural assumptions in order to see your parents more accurately. You'll be learning a new way to relate to them so that you won't expect what they can't give. You'll learn how to protect your emotions and individuality by approaching your parents in a more neutral way—a way they can tolerate emotionally. But first, let's look at a common fantasy that often prevents people from relating to their parents in a realistic way.

The Fantasy That a Parent Will Change

A common fantasy among children of emotionally immature parents is that their parents will have a change of heart and finally love them by showing concern. Unfortunately, self-preoccupied parents refuse all invitations to fulfill their part in their child's healing story. Focused on their own healing fantasy, they expect their children to make up for *their* childhood hurts.

Seeking their parents' healing love, many people hop around after their parents like hungry birds, trying to elicit a crumb of positive response from them. In adulthood, these children often learn a variety of healthy communication skills and hope that these skills will improve their relationship with their parents. They think they might finally have the techniques necessary to draw their parents into a rewarding interaction.

————Annie's Story————

Annie's mother, Betty, a woman with strong religious convictions, had always been emotionally insensitive, and her childhood treatment of Annie sometimes verged on physical and emotional abuse. Although Annie had lived with this treatment for a long time, she reached the breaking point when Betty made a derogatory comment about Annie in front of her colleagues at Annie's award ceremony at work. Annie's feelings were deeply hurt, and she was embarrassed in front of her friends. The insult was so blatant that Annie was sure her mother couldn't deny the wildly inappropriate nature and timing of her comment, as she usually did. But Betty wouldn't take responsibility, coldly denying that what she'd done was problematic.

Over the next few days, Annie kept trying to get Betty to understand how hurt she was. She finally wrote a letter to her mother, telling her how she felt and asking her to sit down with her and talk it out. Annie put a great deal of thought into the letter, which was extremely emotionally articulate, in hopes that Betty would see and regret that her behavior had been so chronically insensitive over the years. But Betty didn't offer any response. Emptiness hung between them, along with Annie's impression that her mother couldn't care less.

"I want to say to her, 'I'm your *daughter*,'" Annie cried. "Murderers kill people, and their moms still love them. We're family; she's my mom. How can she just let that go?"

This wasn't the first time Annie had tried to reach Betty emotionally. After starting therapy, Annie tried to express herself and work things out in a healthy way whenever her parents were mean or disrespectful toward her. Although Betty routinely dismissed Annie's outreach, she'd always remained in contact so she could see Annie's three little boys. But this time it was different.

"What I can't get over is that there's *nothing* coming back, not even anger," Annie said. "All I want is some level of response that shows this matters, even if I've just made her angry."

In addition to being wounded, Annie was confused. Although Betty refused to respond, Annie knew her mother was sociable and capable of showing kindness and generosity toward other people. Annie understood that those relationships were more superficial, but this knowledge didn't help her emotionally. "You'd think my mom would have *some* natural desire to make things better between us—some kind of acknowledgment, or maybe even something through Dad." Annie's sorrow and incomprehension showed on her face.

Annie was grieving over not having an emotionally supportive mother, and working through that would take time. But she was also aware that her appeals were making things worse, and it was important to address that too. Annie was confused. She was doing everything she knew to repair the relationship: communicating clearly, making respectful requests, and being emotionally honest. She wondered how they could work anything out without talking about it.

"Annie," I said, "you're doing all the right things in trying to make a connection with your mom. You're looking for emotional intimacy with her, which makes perfect sense, but I don't think she can tolerate it. While you think you're just trying to relate, your mom probably sees it as a major threat to her equilibrium. After all, she's been living like this for years. Your openness and honesty are more than she can handle. Think of it as though your mom has a snake phobia. You keep plopping a big, fat, writhing snake right in her lap. She can't stand it, no matter how meaningful it might be to you." Emotional closeness demanded a level of emotional maturity her mother simply didn't have. But her mother's silence made Annie feel like an emotional hostage. She couldn't rest until her mother was happy with her.

I told Annie that the only way Betty was going to come around was if Annie stopped talking about her misbehavior and how hurtful it was. Annie needed to find a way forward that didn't involve her mother's participation. That's the only thing that works with parents who are terrified of emotional intimacy. I explained that she could have a relationship with her mother, but it wouldn't be the kind of relationship she yearned for. Her best option was to manage their interactions deliberately, rather than seeking emotional intimacy.

Annie was open to my suggestions but still felt confused. She could remember Betty's anguished visits with her own mother, who was also rejecting, when Annie was a child. Betty felt so unloved by her own mother that, after these visits, she was left sobbing with no one to comfort her but Annie. "How could she now be doing this to her own daughter?" Annie asked. "You'd think she'd hate to do that to her own child after she suffered so much." It was a good point, but Betty was just passing her trauma down the line, as people tend to do when they repress their childhood pain.

Annie was so intent on winning her mother's approval that she'd stopped evaluating the relationship. She'd never asked herself whether Betty was the type of person she enjoyed being around.

Forging a New Relationship

The rest of this chapter explores how to handle an emotionally immature parent, as well as other people, by changing your expectations and replacing reactivity with observation. Three key approaches will help you free yourself from getting caught up in your parent's emotional immaturity: detached observation, maturity awareness, and stepping away from your old role-self.

Detached Observation

The first step in gaining your emotional freedom is to assess whether either of your parents was emotionally immature. Given that you're still reading this book, you've probably decided that at least one of your parents fits that description. Such a parent can probably never fulfill your childhood vision of a loving parent. The only achievable goal is to act from your own true nature, not the role-self that pleases your parent. You can't win your parent over, but you can save yourself.

For my own understanding of how this works, I'm indebted to family therapist Murray Bowen for his family systems theory (1978), which describes how emotionally immature parents promote emotional enmeshment over individual identity. As a reminder, enmeshment occurs when parents don't respect boundaries, project their unresolved issues onto their children, and get too involved in their children's business. In families dominated by emotionally immature people, enmeshment and playing roles are valued in order to keep the family "close." Of course, genuine communication and emotional intimacy are absent in such families. No one's true self is ever acknowledged. Further, in an enmeshed family, if you have a problem with someone, you talk about that person to other people instead of going to the person directly. Bowen called this triangling and characterized enmeshment as the glue that keeps such families together.

Bowen also explored how this situation might be remedied, at least for some family members. He found that observation and emotional detachment can give individuals a place to stand outside of their family system. When people keep themselves poised in neutral observation, they can't be hurt or emotionally ensnared by other people's behavior.

Becoming Observational

When interacting with emotionally immature people, you'll feel more centered if you operate from a calm, thinking perspective, rather than emotional reactivity. Start by settling yourself and getting into an observational, detached frame of mind. There are any number of ways to do this. For example, you can count your breaths slowly, tense and relax your muscle groups in a systematic sequence, or imagine calming imagery.

Next, your job is to stay detached emotionally and observe how others behave, just like a scientist would. Pretend you're conducting an anthropological field study. What words would you use to describe others' facial expressions? What is their body language communicating? Does their voice sound calm or tense? Do they appear rigid or receptive? How do they respond when you try to relate? What do you find yourself feeling? Can you spot any of the emotionally immature behaviors described in chapters 2 and 3?

If you're practicing observing your parent or other loved ones and find yourself getting emotional, your distress is a sign that your healing fantasy has been activated. You've fallen back into believing that you can't be okay if they don't validate you. If you start slipping into your fantasy that you may be able to get the other person to change, you'll feel weak, vulnerable, apprehensive, and needy. This extremely unpleasant feeling of weakness is a signal that you need to shift out of responding emotionally and move back into observing mode.

If you find yourself becoming reactive, silently repeat to yourself, "Detach, detach, detach." Make a point of consciously describing the other person in words—silently and to yourself. During a stressful interaction, this kind of mental narration can center and ground you. Whenever you try to find the exact words to describe something, it helps redirect your brain's energy away from emotional reactivity. The same goes for getting control over your own emotional reactions. Silently narrating your own emotional reactions can give you that extra bit of objectivity that cools things down.

If the other person is still getting to you, find an excuse to put some distance between you. Excuse yourself from the room for a bathroom break, play with a pet, take a walk, or run an errand. Gaze out the window and notice nature. If you're interacting on the phone, find a pretext to get off the phone and say you look forward to talking another time. Use whatever excuse you need to take some time to get yourself back into a more detached, observational mind-set.

As you can see, staying observational isn't passive; it's a very active process. It's also the royal road out of emotional enmeshment. As you practice observing, you'll become stronger and more confident in your ability to see what's really going on, especially now that you have more of an understanding of emotional immaturity. You no longer have to be the upset, helpless child, devastated by potshots from your parent. Your clear mind and observational attitude will keep you strong no matter what the other person does.

Relatedness vs. Relationship

Observing allows you to stay in a state of relatedness with your parents or other loved ones without getting caught up in their emotional tactics and expectations about how you should be. *Relatedness* is different from *relationship*. In relatedness, there's communication but no goal of having a satisfying emotional exchange. You stay in contact, handle others as you need to, and have whatever interactions are tolerable without exceeding the limits that work for you.

In contrast, engaging in a real relationship means being open and establishing emotional reciprocity. If you try this with emotionally immature people, you'll feel frustrated and invalidated. As soon as you start looking for emotional understanding from such people, you won't be as balanced within yourself. It makes more sense to aim for simple relatedness with them, saving your relationship aspirations for people who can give something back.

The Maturity Awareness Approach

Once you've gotten the hang of being observational rather than relationship oriented, you can turn your attention to maturity awareness. This approach will grant you emotional freedom from painful relationships by taking the emotional maturity of others into account. Estimating the probable maturity level of the person you're dealing with is one of the best ways to take care of yourself in any interaction. Once you peg a person's maturity level, his or her responses will make more sense and be more predictable.

If you determine that the other person is showing emotional immaturity as described in chapters 2 and 3, there are three ways to relate to the person without getting yourself upset:

1. Expressing and then letting go

2. Focusing on the outcome, not the relationship

3. Managing, not engaging

Expressing and Then Letting Go

Tell the other person what you want to say in as calm and nonjudgmental a way as you can, and don't try to control the outcome. Explicitly say what you feel or want and enjoy that act of self-expression, but release any need for the other person to hear you or change. You can't force others to empathize or understand. The point is to feel good about yourself for engaging in what I call clear, intimate communication. Others may or may not respond how you want them to, but that doesn't matter. What matters is that you expressed your true thoughts and feelings in a calm, clear way. That goal is achievable and within your control.

Focusing on the Outcome, Not the Relationship

Ask yourself what you're really trying to get from the other person in this interaction. Be honest. If it's your parent, do you want your parent to listen to you? Understand you? Regret his or her behavior? Apologize to you? Make amends?

If your goal involves empathy or a change of heart on your parent's part, stop right there and come up with a different goal—one that's specific and achievable. Remember, you can't expect immature, emotionally phobic people to be different from how they are. However, you can set a specific goal for the interaction.

Identify the specific outcome you want from each interaction and set it as a goal. Here are some examples: "I express myself to my mother even though I'm nervous." "I tell my parents I'm not coming home for Christmas." "I ask my father to talk nicely to my children." Your goal might be just to express your feelings. This is achievable because you can ask others to listen, even though you can't make them understand. Or your goal might be as simple as reaching an agreement about where the family will have Thanksgiving dinner. The key is to go into the interaction always knowing the end point you wish to arrive at.

Let me be crystal clear: focus on the outcome, not the relationship. As soon as you focus on the relationship and try to improve it or change it at an emotional level, an interaction with an emotionally immature person will deteriorate. The person will regress emotionally and attempt to control you so that you'll stop upsetting him or her. If you keep the focus on a specific question or outcome, you're more likely to contact the person's adult side.

Of course, if you're dealing with an empathetic person it's healthy to address emotional issues in the relationship. With emotionally mature people, you can talk about your feelings honestly, and they'll share their feelings and thoughts with you as well. As long as both people have enough emotional maturity, this kind of clear, intimate communication will result in knowing each other better and feeling emotionally nourished.

Managing, Not Engaging

Instead of emotionally engaging with immature people, set a goal of managing the interaction, including duration and topics. You may need to repeatedly redirect the conversation where you want it to go. Gently ease past attempts to change the topic or bait you emotionally. Be polite, but be prepared to address the issue as many times as it takes to get a clear answer. Emotionally immature people don't have a good strategy for countering another person's persistence. Their attempts at diversion and avoidance ultimately break down if you keep asking the same question. As a reminder, also manage your own emotions by observing and narrating your feelings to yourself, rather than becoming reactive.

Some Common Concerns About the Maturity Awareness Approach

People who hear about this approach for the first time tend to have certain concerns about it, especially about using it with their parents. Here are a few that I hear most often, with a response to each.

Concern: This sounds like a cold and unrewarding way to have a relationship with my parents. I don't want to be thinking every second I'm with them.

Response: If things are going well and you're enjoying being with your parents, there's no need to use this approach. But if you're getting emotional, angry, or disappointed, it's best to switch over to observing objectively and managing the interaction. You aren't being cold; you're focusing on what helps you maintain emotional balance.

Concern: I feel guilty and devious when I keep some mental distance from my parents. I want to be open and natural with them.

Response: Observing consciously doesn't mean being devious or deceptive; it means keeping yourself from being drawn into a whirlpool of reactions that make things worse for everybody. As an adult, you want to be able to think as an individual, including amidst interactions with other people. Having clear self-awareness doesn't mean you're being disloyal.

Concern: It's all very nice to advocate not being emotional around your parents, but you haven't seen how intense and manipulative my parents can be! I get overwhelmed by the intensity of their reactions.

Response: We can all get overwhelmed by another person's emotion. That's known as emotional contagion. But you'll feel more secure if you set an intention of observing what's happening, rather than becoming swept up in it. Even a bit of observation will help lift you out of the pressure to feel others' distress. It's *their* distress, not yours. You might feel some of it, but you don't have to become as distressed as they are.

Concern: My parents have been very good to me. They paid for my education and loaned me money. I would feel disrespectful if I saw them as emotionally immature. It doesn't seem right to think about them this way.

Response: There's nothing right or wrong about thoughts. You aren't being disrespectful by being truthful with yourself about your parents' emotional limitations. To be an emotionally mature adult, you must be free to observe and assess others in the privacy of your own mind. It isn't disloyal to have your own opinion.

You can respect your parents for everything they've given you, but you don't have to pretend they have no human frailties. As we discussed in chapter 2, satisfying a child's physical and financial needs is not the same as meeting that child's emotional needs. For instance, if you needed someone to listen—to provide essential emotional connection—receiving money or a good education might distract you from that need, but it wouldn't fill it.

Concern: How in the world do I stay calm and keep observing when my parents are making me feel guilty?

Response: Center yourself by focusing on your breath as it flows in and out. Feeling guilty isn't an emergency. Observe what's going on and silently narrate it to yourself in specific words. Mentally describing what's happening helps move you from your brain's emotional centers to its more objective, logical areas. Another strategy is to count. How many seconds did your parent go on that time? You might look at a clock and decide how much longer you're willing to listen. When that time is up, interrupt politely and say you have to leave or get off the phone soon. Say you have something to do, then disengage. You can also talk kindly to yourself: *There's no reason to feel guilt. They're trying to push their feelings on me. I haven't done anything wrong. I have a right to an opinion.* Try reminding yourself that your parent is attempting a diversion, and that it's just like dealing with an upset toddler: the unpleasantness will be over sooner if you stay calm and focused on your desired outcome instead of getting into the fray.

Concern: I can learn and practice these skills while I'm sitting calmly by myself, but it all goes out the window when my parents start criticizing me. I feel as nervous as a placekicker in the Super Bowl. How can I ever be calm enough to observe or manage them?

Response: The Super Bowl placekicker may be nervous, but you can be sure he's working to be as calm as he can. A big part of sports psychology is learning how to relax when under stress. Your goal is to practice being a little less nervous than usual by focusing on the outcome you want. This isn't the Super Bowl. There's no pressure, because you are no longer struggling to gain anything. You don't need the negativity your parents dish up. It isn't about winning or losing; it's about freeing yourself from reacting to your parents' emotional contagion.

Concern: I worry so much about my parents. They're always unhappy about something. I just want to make them feel better.

Response: You can't. Have you noticed that no matter what you do, your parents don't stay happy for long? Just because they're complaining doesn't necessarily mean their goal is to feel better. That's your interpretation. Treat them nicely, but don't bleed for them. Their healing story and role-selves may require a lot of suffering and complaining. It isn't your job to abandon your own path and try to push them from behind. If you do, they're likely to become even more difficult and unpleasant.

−Annie's Story Continued−

After months of enduring her mother Betty's stubborn silent treatment, Annie tried the maturity awareness approach. She invited her parents to join her at one of the kids' soccer games. That was about as long as Annie thought she could stay objective and in control emotionally. Her desired outcome was a visit with no drama, simply reestablishing contact with her parents. Instead of trying to engage Betty in an openhearted way, Annie stayed in a neutral observing mode, interacting pleasantly but not expecting any warmth from her mother. Her parents came late, as usual, and Annie greeted them nicely, saying "Hey, I'm glad you're here."

Annie gave Betty a little hug and offered her a snack. Betty looked upset and emotional—again making herself the center of their interaction—but as Annie reported, "I didn't acknowledge it or feed it." Annie was able to let go of her attempts to establish emotional intimacy with Betty because she now understood that Betty's emotion was probably about herself and didn't reflect a desire to engage with Annie. Indeed, Betty hardly spoke to Annie during the game.

As they were leaving the game, Betty choked up but still didn't talk to Annie. Annie was mentally prepared, and rather than feeling irritated, she simply observed how Betty avoided genuine communication and instead acted like she was the injured party.

Afterward, Annie summed up her experience with her mother by saying, "I'm finally figuring out that this is who my mother is—this is her personality. It's not about me. I'm glad I didn't get sucked into how *she's* the one who's been hurt. I'm proud that I'm able to separate her behavior from my sense of worth."

On Betty's birthday, Annie called and left a couple of messages, but she didn't invite her mother over. Annie felt good about doing as much as was emotionally possible for her to do. She didn't make it her problem that Betty didn't call back. When Annie finally reached Betty on the phone a few days later, her mother answered tersely, in a cold, reserved tone. Annie played it straight and said, "I'm surprised I didn't hear from you. Did you get my messages?" When Betty answered coolly in the affirmative, not thanking her and not showing any warmth, Annie decided to end the conversation and said, "We'll have to catch up sometime, Mom. Why don't you call me? We'll schedule a get-together."

After that conversation, Annie felt more emotionally free. She was no longer obsessed with her mother's rejection. She'd managed to relate to Betty as a fellow adult, instead of playing out the old role-self of an openhearted little girl who hoped to one day win her disapproving mother's love.

In our next session, she said, "I no longer feel that I've done anything wrong. It's sad that this important relationship, which I've always struggled with, won't have a good resolution. But the fact that my mother doesn't respond doesn't put a judgment on me; it's just another indication that she can't handle a close relationship with me. Even if my warmth repels her that badly, I can't switch it off. I don't *want* to switch my warmth off."

Stepping Out of an Old Role-Self

The ability to step back and observe not only your parent but also your own role-self is where emotional freedom begins. When you see how you've gotten stuck in a role-self and are trying to make a healing fantasy come true, you can decide to do it differently.

———Rochelle's Story———

Rochelle's mother was a very demanding woman who expected Rochelle to be at her beck and call. As Rochelle put it, "I used to feel like I couldn't be okay unless my mother changed and acknowledged me." But when Rochelle decided to observe her mother's emotional immaturity instead of being automatically hurt by it, she felt a profound change: "For the first time, I saw her behavior for what it was. I didn't get angry or disappointed, like before, when I felt like I *had* to get her to acknowledge me." Because Rochelle had worked on acknowledging herself and her genuine feelings toward her mother, she no longer felt like she had to play a certain role or fulfill her mother's healing fantasy by pouring attention on her. "I no longer feel compelled to jump in immediately and be the 'good daughter' for her. I don't have to take on her problems." Rochelle now calls her mother when she feels like it, and she feels free now to say no to her mother's requests. And now that she doesn't feel obligated to put on the role-self of the dutiful daughter, Rochelle actually feels free to be more relaxed around her mom.

Keeping a Grip on Your Own Thoughts and Feelings

The ultimate goal in any interaction with a parent or an emotionally immature person is to keep a grip on your own mind and feelings. To do this, you need to stay observational, noticing how you're feeling and how the other person is acting. From this perspective, you can retain your individual point of view and be more immune to the other person's emotional contagion.

With parents, keeping your mind on your specific desired outcome for the interaction will help you retain an objective, observing stance no matter how they behave. It keeps you in your thinking brain, instead of falling into your emotions or a fight-or-flight reaction. In this way, focusing on your goal for the interaction helps you hold on to your true self while old healing fantasies and role expectations are swirling around you.

Being Cautious About New Openness

According to Murray Bowen (1978), as a child becomes more of an individual, the emotionally immature parent's knee-jerk reaction is to do something that attempts to force the child back into an enmeshed pattern. If the child doesn't take the bait, such parents may ultimately start relating in a more genuine way.

I advise caution if your parents show uncharacteristic openness in response to your adoption of an observational and goal-directed approach. If they start treating you with more respect or open up a bit, you could be vulnerable to getting sucked back into your old healing fantasy (*They're finally going to give me what I need*). Be careful! Your inner child will always hope that your parents will finally change and offer what you've always longed for. But your job is to keep your adult outlook and continue relating to them as a separate, independent adult. At this point, you're looking for an adult relationship with them, not a re-creation of parent-child dynamics, right?

If you allow yourself to slip back into those old childhood hopes, your parents' increased openness is likely to evaporate instantly because you'll no longer feel safe to them. Remember, your parents are probably emotionally phobic and unable to handle genuine intimacy. If you become more open, they'll react by pulling back, trying to get you off balance and back under their control. This is the only way such people know to protect themselves from the vulnerability of too much closeness.

In the end, the overall dynamic remains the same. Your parents will be emotionally available to you in inverse proportion to how much you feel the need for them. Only if you operate from your adult, objective mind will you feel safe to your parents. It's unfortunate, but the reality is, they are simply too terrified to handle your inner child's emotional needs.

In your interactions, just keep observing the present moment, and then follow the inclinations of your true nature. Your true self knows everyone involved and the reality of the situation, so it's likely to come up with exactly the response that's needed. But the only way the true self can do that is if you stay in an objective, watchful state that's grounded in your own individuality.

Summary

Our early dependence on our parents makes us seek their love and attention. However, we must step away from our childhood roles if we don't want to repeat them in our adult relationships. The maturity awareness approach will help you deal with an emotionally immature parent—or any difficult, self-involved person—more effectively. You'll have better results if you try to *relate* to your parent in a neutral way, rather than trying to have a *relationship*. First, you need to assess your parent's level of maturity and approach interactions between the two of you from an observational perspective—focusing on thinking, rather than reacting emotionally. Then you can employ the three steps involved in the maturity awareness approach: expressing yourself and then letting it go; focusing on the outcome rather than the relationship; and managing the interaction rather than engaging emotionally.

In the next chapter, we'll explore the road to freedom from old parent-child patterns. As you read on, you'll see how good it feels to finally step out of old patterns of relating that have been running your life.

Chapter 9

How It Feels to Live Free of Roles and Fantasies

I n this chapter, we'll explore what life feels like when you stop playing a role in order to relate to an emotionally immature parent. We'll see how new thoughts and actions can help you transcend the emotional loneliness of playing a role as you regain the emotional freedom to truly be yourself. As you'll learn, it can be a struggle to get free, but it's well worth it.

Family Patterns That May Be Holding You Back

Before we dive into discovering and fostering your true self, let's review some of the family dynamics that keep people trapped in old roles.

Discouragement of Individuality

If you were raised by an emotionally immature parent, you spent your early years tiptoeing around the anxieties of an emotionally phobic person. The enmeshed families created by such parents are a stronghold against their fear of individuality. A child's individuality is seen as a threat to emotionally insecure and immature parents because it stirs up fears about possible rejection or abandonment. If you think independently, you might criticize them or decide to leave. They feel much safer seeing family members as predictable fantasy characters rather than real individuals.

For parents who fear both real emotion and abandonment, authenticity in their children presents frightening evidence of the child's individuality. These parents feel threatened when their children express genuine emotions because it makes interactions unpredictable and seems threatening to family ties. Therefore their children, in an attempt to prevent their parents from becoming anxious, often suppress any authentic thoughts, feelings, or desires that would disturb their parents' sense of security.

Denial of Individual Needs and Preferences

Parents who need to keep strict control because of their anxieties often teach their children not only how they should do things, but also how they should feel and think. Children who are internalizers tend to take this instruction to heart and may come to believe that their unique inner experiences have no legitimacy. Such parents teach their children to be ashamed of any aspect of themselves that differs from their parents. In this way, children may come to see their uniqueness, and even their strengths, as odd and unlovable.

In such families, internalizing children often learn to feel ashamed of the following normal behaviors:

- Enthusiasm

- Spontaneity

- Sadness and grief over hurt, loss, or change

- Uninhibited affection

- Saying what they really feel and think

- Expressing anger when they feel wronged or slighted

On the other hand, they are taught that the following experiences and feelings are acceptable or even desirable:

- Obedience and deference toward authority

- Physical illness or injury that puts the parent in a position of strength and control

- Uncertainty and self-doubt

- Liking the same things as the parent

- Guilt and shame over imperfections or being different

- Willingness to listen, especially to the parent's distress and complaints

- Stereotyped gender roles, typically people-pleasing in girls and toughness in boys

If you were an internalizing child with an emotionally immature parent, you were taught many self-defeating things about how to get along in life. Here are some of the biggest ones:

- Give first consideration to what other people want you to do.

- Don't speak up for yourself.

- Don't ask for help.

- Don't want anything for yourself.

Internalizing children of emotionally immature parents learn that "goodness" means being as self-effacing as possible so their parents can get their needs met first. Internalizers come to see their feelings and needs as unimportant at best and shameful at worst. However, once they become conscious of how distorted this mind-set is, things can change rather quickly.

For example, Carolyn's healing fantasy was that if she was subservient and let her mother be the main character in her life story, her mother would finally appreciate her. But in therapy she came to this realization: "My family role was a fiction. I've realized I'm not a bit character in someone else's novel—I can step off the page. I no longer want be in that book."

Adhering to an Internalized Parental Voice

You may wonder how parents can manage to train a child to go against his or her gut instincts and life-affirming impulses. It occurs through a process I call parent-voice internalization. As children, we absorb our parents' opinions and beliefs in the form of an inner voice that keeps up an ongoing commentary that appears to be coming from inside us. Often this voice says things like "You should…," "You'd better…," or "You have to…," but it may just as frequently make unkind comments about your worth, intelligence, or moral character.

Although this commentary sounds like your own voice, it's really an echo of your early caretakers. If you'd like to learn more about this, the book *Conquer Your Critical Inner Voice* (Firestone, Firestone, and Catlett 2002) can help you identify where your inner voices came from and how to free yourself from their negative influence.

Everyone internalizes their parents' voices; it's how we're socialized. And while some people end up with a supportive, friendly, problem-solving inner commentary, many hear only angry, critical, or contemptuous voices. The unrelenting presence of these negative messages can do more damage than the parent him- or herself. Therefore, you need to interrupt these voices in the act of making you feel bad so that you can separate your self-worth from their critical evaluations. The goal is to recognize the voice as something imported that isn't part of your true self, so that it no longer feels like a natural part of your own thinking. One way of doing so is to use the maturity awareness approach in chapter 8 to relate to those negative voices inside your head just as you'd use that approach with a parent.

As you get more objective about your emotionally immature parent, you can also reevaluate the voices in your head and begin to free yourself from their undue influence. Just as with your actual parent, you can make a point to observe how these internal voices talk to you. You can take what you hear with a grain of salt and make a rational decision about whether you want to keep listening to that inner critic.

Freedom to Be Human and Imperfect

Internalized parental voices probably originate in the left hemisphere of the brain, where language and logic rule. When the left brain is allowed to run the show, it puts perfectionism and efficiency before feeling, and judgment before compassion (McGilchrist 2009). Without the balance provided by the more personal and intuitive right side of the brain, your left brain will use machinelike equations of right and wrong to size you up. Its moralistic voice will tell you that you're either good or bad, perfect or broken, depending on what you accomplish. This kind of judgmental logic is an aspect of the mental rigidity that accompanies emotional immaturity.

———Jason's Story———

Jason, a successful college professor and amateur artist, had been depressed for years. He'd grown up with an arrogant, critical father and a self-preoccupied mother, neither of whom had any patience for him.

Jason had internalized a very negative, perfectionistic inner parental voice that constantly evaluated him. No matter what Jason did, that inner voice had something deflating to say about it. Anytime he failed to perform as perfectly as that inner voice demanded, he instantly reacted with self-judgment and self-loathing. In addition, he could never tell if he really wanted to do something or just thought he wanted to because the voice said he should.

Fortunately, in the course of therapy, Jason became aware of the connection between this inner voice and his disapproving parents. Like his parents, this negative voice criticized all his choices, constantly undermining his self-confidence. Instead of accepting it as the voice of reason, as he had for years, Jason finally recognized it as the disembodied voice of his parents and understood its destructive agenda.

Once he was able to hear the voice for what it was, Jason realized that he didn't have to believe it when it told him he was being bad, selfish, or lazy. Instead of forcing himself to do things perfectly because the voice told him to, he started asking himself questions to clarify his own desires. When he felt dread about doing something, instead of forcing himself to do it, Jason paused and asked himself, *Are my needs part of this picture? Am I the biggest part of the picture? And what's the balance between my own needs and what the voice is saying I have to do?*

Jason had lived his whole adult life approaching tasks with the thought *Oh damn, I have to do this.* Now he saw more alternatives, asking himself, *Do I really have to do it right now? And if it's necessary, how and when am I going to fit in the other things I want to do?* He learned to first ask himself what he wanted to do, making choices on his own behalf and beating the inner voice to the punch. By taking a moment to deliberately think about what he really wanted, Jason was at last freeing himself from the tyranny of his inner voice.

Freedom to Have Your Genuine Thoughts and Feelings

If your childhood thoughts and feelings made your parents uncomfortable, you would have quickly learned to suppress these inner experiences. Knowing your true emotions and thoughts probably felt dangerous if it threatened to distance you from the people you depended on. You learned that your goodness or badness lay not only in your behavior, but in your mind as well. In this way, you may have learned the absurd idea that you can be a bad person for having certain thoughts and feelings, and you may still hold that belief.

However, you need access to all your inner experiences, without feeling guilty or ashamed of them. Plus, you'll have more energy when you let your thoughts and feelings flow naturally, without worrying about what they mean about you. A thought or feeling means nothing more than that you're having a thought or feeling. Regaining the freedom to simply let your thoughts and feelings come and go without condemnation is a profound relief.

The fact is, having a thought or feeling isn't initially under your control. You don't plan to think or feel things; you just do. Think of it this way: Your thoughts and feelings are an organic part of nature expressing itself through you. Nature isn't going to be dishonest about how you feel, and you don't have a choice about what thoughts nature brings up in you. Accepting the truth of your feelings and thoughts doesn't make you a bad person. It makes you a *whole* person, and mature enough to know your own mind.

Freedom to Suspend Contact

Ideally, you'd probably like to have the freedom to be yourself yet protect yourself while continuing to relate to your parent. Still, you might find it necessary at times to protect your emotional health by suspending contact for a while. Although this can stir up tremendous guilt and self-doubt, consider the possibility that you may have good reasons for keeping your distance. For example, your parent may be emotionally hurtful or disrespect your boundaries—an intrusive way of relating that impinges upon your right to your own identity. You may want to take a break from dealing with a parent who behaves in this way.

Some parents are so unreflective that, despite repeated explanations, they simply don't accept that their behavior is problematic. In addition, some sadistic parents truly are malevolent toward their children, and enjoy the pain and frustration they cause. Children of these sorts of parents may decide that suspending contact is the best solution. Just because a person is your biological parent doesn't mean you have to keep an emotional or social tie to that person.

Fortunately, you don't need to have an active relationship with your parents to free yourself from their influence. If this weren't so, people wouldn't be able to emotionally separate from parents who live far away or have died. True freedom from unhealthy roles and relationships starts *within* each of us, not in our interactions and confrontations with others.

————Aisha's Story————

Aisha, a twenty-seven-year-old woman with a successful career in TV reporting, struggled with depression and low self-esteem.

Her mother, Ella, had always called Aisha a problem child. Although Ella doted on Aisha's little brother, she was critical and exacting toward Aisha. Aisha felt she could never please Ella, but she kept trying to make her proud anyway. However, Ella kept harping on the things Aisha didn't do perfectly. Ella also couldn't resist mocking Aisha in front of other people, including her boyfriends.

Although Aisha confronted Ella about these behaviors many times, it never seemed to help. Ella always feigned innocence and even used Aisha's tears and anger as further proof that she was a bad child who treated her mother poorly. Aisha became so sensitized to Ella's derogatory comments that a simple dinner together often deteriorated into tears before the evening was over.

Once Aisha decided to break off contact with Ella, her stress levels decreased markedly. No longer exposed to hurtful interactions with Ella, Aisha felt happier than she ever had. She worried that she was a bad person for not seeing her mother, but she couldn't deny how much better she felt and how much more self-esteem she had without Ella in her life. Aisha's boyfriend even remarked on how much more relaxed she seemed.

Months later, Aisha brought a card from her mother to a therapy session to read to me. Although Ella clearly meant it as a plea to resume contact, for Aisha her mother's words only confirmed why she needed to keep her distance. In an act of pure self-justification, Ella had only written about her feelings and how she'd never done anything but love Aisha. She showed no empathy for Aisha and didn't take any responsibility for her hurtful behavior.

Aisha had explained her hurt feelings to her mother many times. There was no mystery about why Aisha had broken off contact. Any mystery existed only in Ella's mind. Her idealized fantasy of being a loving mother simply didn't leave any room for Aisha's feelings to exist.

Freedom to Set Limits and Choose How Much to Give

While suspending contact is sometimes necessary, some people are able to set limits so effectively that their parents simply don't have an opportunity to do more harm. One way to do this is to take control of how frequently you're in contact with your parents. By setting limits on contacts, you can devote more energy to your own needs for self-care. Your parents may protest when you aren't as generous with your time or attention as you used to be; however, these difficult moments present a priceless opportunity to get over any irrational guilt for having needs of your own.

Remember, if you're an internalizer, you'll be inclined to feel that the answer to any problem is for you to make things better, and that if you try a little harder, the situation—including others' behavior—will improve. It's such a relief to realize that this isn't true. More often, internalizers keep trying harder and externalizers keep taking advantage of this. Remember, your goodness as a person isn't based on how much you give in relationships, and it isn't selfish to set limits on people who keep on taking. Your job is to take care of yourself, regardless of what others think you should be doing for them.

Paying attention to subtle energy drains from other people can help you realize when you're giving too much. Even in minor encounters, you can adjust how much you give so you won't be exhausted by trying to fulfill others' needs.

I recommend using the maturity awareness mind-set to observe how your parents react when you ask them to respect your boundaries. Notice whether they try to make you feel ashamed and guilty, as if they have a right to do whatever they want, regardless of how it affects you.

————Brad's Story————

Brad had his hands full with a demanding job, four children, and a shaky marriage. Although he was under a lot of stress, he agreed to let his irascible mother, Ruth, move in with his family after she lost the lease on her apartment following an argument with her landlord. Soon after Ruth moved in, Brad discovered that his wife had been having an affair, which almost destroyed their marriage. Around the same time, Brad's teenage daughter was caught smoking pot at school. Ruth showed no sensitivity to the tension in the house. In fact, she added to it by expressing her opinions whenever she felt like it. If she felt snubbed, she would slam doors, yell at the children, and swear at the pets. Brad felt like he was nearing a breakdown.

Brad saw that he had to choose between his health and his mother's sense of entitlement. He'd repeatedly tried talking to Ruth about her behavior, but it hadn't helped. Ruth continued to try to rule the roost and was often unpleasant to Brad's children and their friends. Brad finally asked Ruth to move into a rental townhouse they owned on the other side of town.

Ruth was stunned. She never saw it coming, just as she never understood why her landlord insisted she leave. Brad was tactful but remained firm. Predictably, Ruth erupted with "You don't love me!"

Brad kept to the subject: "We don't have to have a big scene to have a change of circumstances. We love you, but it's time for you to go. It isn't our job to take care of you. You are capable of caring for yourself."

"Are you going to charge me rent?" his mother asked.

"Yes, and we'll have to charge you more if you want to include utilities."

In our next session, Brad reviewed this encounter and described how he didn't let himself get needled. Instead, he told himself, *I'm not going there this time*, and kept his focus on the outcome he wanted from the talk: for Ruth to move out.

Brad had finally realized how much stress Ruth was adding to an already difficult living situation: "With her in the house, my blood pressure felt like it was sky-high. I used to tell myself to make it work, but the fact is I don't *want* to make it work with her. I have the energy, but it's not what I *want* to do." Brad had started seeing things differently: "Being a member of a family doesn't give anybody free rein to treat people like crap."

Freedom to Have Self-Compassion

In order to take care of yourself, you need to feel compassion for yourself (McCullough et al. 2003). Knowing your own feelings and having sympathy for yourself are two basic building blocks of strong individuality. Only if you have self-compassion will you know when to set limits or stop giving excessively.

Extending compassion to yourself can be so healing, yet it can also feel quite unnatural at first. One woman described it this way: "I looked back on that little girl I was and saw that she went through a lot. For the first time, I felt bad for myself. It was like exhaling after discovering that I'd been holding my breath for a long, long time. It's an odd feeling: sad, intense, relieving—so many things at once. Now I have empathy for how painful and exhausting my childhood was. Looking at myself as a little girl was like an out-of-body experience. I was finally able to say, 'Wow, poor girl,' which I've never said before."

Another woman felt this kind of self-compassion when she came across an old school photo of herself. She found herself speaking to the girl in the photo, saying, "You brave girl, you're smiling for the school picture, but you had so much to deal with."

Grief and tears are a normal response to the dawning of self-compassion, arising as we come to grips with painful truths that are hard to take in. If you've spent many years not being validated, you've probably suppressed sadness more than any other emotion. Daniel Siegel, a well-known psychiatrist and author, has written eloquently about the healing power of emotion (2009). He says that if we allow ourselves to sit with our true feelings as they emerge, we can be transformed. Feeling deep emotion is our way of processing important new information. Being conscious of our emotions, including grief, is how we do the inner work of psychological growth.

According to Siegel, when we are feeling emotion, we are integrating and absorbing new awareness into our consciousness (2009). I often tell clients that tears can be thought of as a physical sign of the integration process that's occurring in our hearts and minds. When you cry these deeper tears of realization, you ultimately end up feeling better. This kind of crying helps you develop into a more integrated and complex person, and will leave you feeling more settled and able to regroup.

Regaining the ability to feel for yourself comes in waves, and some of these waves can be very intense. Having a lot of unprocessed emotion to integrate can feel overwhelming. You'll benefit from reaching out to a compassionate friend or therapist for comfort and support to help you through these times, but don't be afraid of this natural process. Your body knows how to cry and grieve. If you let your feelings arise and keep trying to understand them, you'll come out of the experience a more integrated, mature person, with greater compassion for both yourself and others.

Freedom from Excessive Empathy

Internalizers are so emotionally sensitive that they can go overboard in feeling empathy for other people's problems or what they imagine other people's suffering to be. Sometimes they end up feeling worse about another person's situation than the other person does. With healthy empathy, on the other hand, you can have compassion without losing awareness of your own limits.

————Rebecca's Story————

Rebecca's elderly mother, Irene, was an externalizer who complained constantly. Nothing was ever right, even though Rebecca had tried her hardest to make her happy. Although Rebecca was doing a good job of setting boundaries with Irene, she still had a blind spot. One day in session, Rebecca revealed a fundamental error in her thinking when she commented, "But there's nothing wrong with wanting her to feel better."

"Yes, there is!" I found myself exclaiming. This belief was at the heart of Rebecca's self-sacrificing role with her mother. Being invested in Irene feeling better *was* a serious problem because it fueled Rebecca's emotional enmeshment with her mom. I asked Rebecca what evidence she had that Irene wanted to feel better. Irene didn't live her life in such a way that she could feel better, and I couldn't see any signs that she was responding well to anything Rebecca was doing. Feeling better clearly didn't seem to be Irene's goal, so the fact that Rebecca had made it her central agenda doomed her to failure. She was working toward something Irene didn't seem to want. In fact, Irene's life theme was all about *not* getting what she wanted; who was Rebecca to mess with that?

One evening when Rebecca was about to leave Irene's house after a very frustrating day spent unsuccessfully trying to help her, Irene looked at Rebecca and said, "Just keep coming to see me." Rebecca was flabbergasted. After all she had tried to do to make her mother happy, was this all she really wanted? Rebecca decided to take Irene at her word, reining in her empathy and efforts to help so she wouldn't dread visiting her mother. She finally saw that Irene would never be happy, but that this didn't have to be a problem for either of them.

Freedom to Take Action on Your Own Behalf

Growing up with emotionally immature parents may have caused you to feel helpless, both as a child and as an adult. Their lack of emotional attentiveness can make it feel as though what you want doesn't matter. You may have been convinced that all you could do was wait until someone felt like giving you what you need.

It's important to realize that childhood experiences of profound helplessness can feel traumatic, causing people to later react to adult feelings of helplessness with sensations of collapse and a feeling of "There's nothing I can do, and no one will help me." As children, sensitive internalizers can be so affected by this feeling that later they're prone to feeling like victims with no control, at the mercy of powerful people who refuse to give them what they desperately need.

Even if this victim reaction is deeply ingrained, you can always reclaim your right to ask for help—and even more importantly, to keep on asking for help as often as necessary. Action on your own behalf is the antidote to traumatic feelings of helplessness. Although being raised by emotionally immature parents gave you a very limited sampling of what life and relationships have to offer, hopefully you're starting to realize how expansive the possibilities are, and that you owe it to yourself to ask for what you need.

Carissa's Story

After finally seeing how her dominating father, Bob, had trained her to feel helpless and passive around authority figures, Carissa went to visit her parents, prepared to observe them, express herself, manage interactions, and work toward outcomes she wanted. She was amazed at how well the visit went. Thanks to some help from her husband, Alejandro, her father didn't manage to take the floor with his political rants and lectures about his pet peeves. As soon as her father began to warm to his subject, Alejandro suddenly started talking about a different topic—an unexpected turn of events that seemed to confuse Bob and derailed his conversation.

Another time, as her family gathered on the deck for drinks, everyone took their seats in such a way that Bob was about to end up on one side of the deck, facing everyone else on the other side—a perfect setup for activating his proclivity to lecture to a captive audience. Carissa saw it happening and took action. She later told me, "In the past, I would have just thought, *Oh, I'm screwed. Now I'm stuck.* But this time I took charge." She slid her chair next to her dad to prevent him from becoming the center of attention. It worked, allowing conversation to flow around the group, rather than everyone being subjected to a torrent from her father. Using the maturity awareness approach, Carissa had managed the interaction to achieve the outcome she wanted: equal participation.

Freedom to Express Yourself

Expressing yourself with emotionally immature people is an important act of self-affirmation, one that implicitly stakes your claim to exist as an individual, with your own feelings and thoughts. Remember, an important step in the maturity awareness approach is expressing yourself—and then letting go.

It's important to relinquish the belief that if your parents loved you, they'd understand you. As an independent adult, you can function without their understanding. You may not ever have the kind of relationship you've wanted with your parents, but you can make each interaction with them more satisfying for you. You can speak up politely when you feel like it, and be different without offering excuses. By expressing yourself to your parents in this way, you can be authentic even in the absence of their understanding. The point of expressing your feelings is to be true to yourself, not to change your parents. And there's always the likelihood that they can still love you even if they don't get you at all.

Holly's Story

Holly's father, Mel, was a barber who lived in a small Southern town, and most of Holly's phone conversations with her father revolved around his community news. Holly, who held a high-level job as a federal investigator, had always longed for her father's recognition of her accomplishments. But when she brought up her job or other high points in her life, Mel seemed to have no idea how to respond to her. Instead, he often abruptly interrupted her to talk about something that had happened to him. Holly continued to tell him about her life because she wanted to connect with him more authentically, but his typical response was lack of interest. Time and again, Holly just let it go, telling herself that she should respect her father.

When Holly was going through difficulties in her job, she called Mel for moral support. But when she was in the middle of telling him what a tough time she was having, he suddenly changed the subject and started talking about the renovation of the county courthouse. This time, Holly was prepared to handle the situation differently by using clear, intimate communication.

"Dad!" she exclaimed, "I'm going to talk about *me* some more. I'm going through a really hard time. I like to hear your news, but this time can you just listen? I need to talk to you." Holly was pleasantly surprised to find that her father accepted her redirection and just listened. Being emotionally immature, Mel simply didn't have the sensitivity to know when not to change the topic. By speaking up, Holly made her needs clear and finally felt heard by her father.

Freedom to Approach Old Relationships in New Ways

Like Carissa and Holly, you can interact with your parents in new ways that shake up old patterns and keep the focus on the outcome you're seeking. By taking it one interaction at a time, you can experiment with setting aside any unrealistic desires for genuine emotional connection or support from your parents. You aren't denying your past; you're just accepting your parents as they are, without expectations.

Sometimes parents will respond to this kind of honesty and neutrality by relating in a more emotionally genuine way. Though it may seem paradoxical, they may open up more once you stop wanting them to change. When you seem strong and they sense that you no longer need their approval, they may be able to relax more. As you stop trying to win their attention, the emotional intensity ebbs to a point where they sometimes can tolerate more openness. Because they're no longer terrified that your needs will trap them in unbearable levels of emotional intimacy, they may be able to respond to you as they would any other adult, with more reasonableness and courtesy.

The catch is that this can only happen if you've truly relinquished the need for a deep relationship with them. And it may not happen even then. But if you can stay true to yourself, detach emotionally, and interact without expectations, you'll be less likely to trigger your parents' defenses against intimacy. And by giving up your healing fantasy about changing your parents, you let them be who they are. When they're no longer under pressure to change, they may be able to treat you differently—or not. Your job is to be okay either way.

Freedom to Not Want Anything from Your Parent

The most painful interactions with emotionally immature parents occur when their children need something from them. Whether it's attention, love, or communication, many neglected children continue to seek some kind of positive emotional regard from their parents well into adulthood, even though their parents aren't the giving type.

Emotionally immature parents commonly promote the myth that parents are the only source of their children's well-being and self-esteem. Many self-involved parents like it when their child is needy and they can be the center of the child's longing. Witnessing their child's dependency makes them feel secure and in control. If the child goes along with this, the parents gain the power to completely control their child's emotional state.

The idea of stepping back and asking yourself whether you really need your parents—or whether they need you to need them—might seem radical. But if it weren't for family roles and fantasies, your parents might not even be the kind of people you'd seek anything from. So consider whether your need for them is real, or whether it might be a holdover from unmet childhood needs. Do they really have something you want *now*?

This question is relevant to relating to any emotionally immature person, whether spouse, friend, or relative. You can get swept up into believing that you're desperate for a relationship with someone even when you actually don't enjoy the interactions the other person has to offer.

Summary

This chapter explored how it feels to break free from roles and expectations designed to please emotionally immature parents. Although you may have learned to reject yourself thanks to an overly critical inner voice that expects perfection, you can reclaim your true self and genuine thoughts and feelings regardless of other people's reactions. You can claim the freedom to express yourself and take action on your own behalf. You're free to extend compassion to yourself and even grieve what you've lost as a result of having emotionally immature parents. You now know that your first job is your own self-care, including setting limits on how much you give, even to the point of suspending contact with your parents if necessary. You no longer have to exhaust yourself with excessive empathy for other people. In addition, you're likely to find that your relationship with your parents becomes more tolerable as you relinquish the need for their emotional acceptance. And as you shed your old family role, you can relate to your parents more honestly, without needing them to change.

In the next chapter, which is the final chapter in the book, we'll take a look at how you can use the maturity awareness approach to find more emotionally mature friends and partners. I'll also offer some pointers on developing new attitudes and values that will promote the possibility of more rewarding and reciprocal relationships in the future.

Chapter 10

How to Identify Emotionally Mature People

The previous chapter explored how you can reclaim your emotional freedom by honoring your true self in your relationships with your parents and others, setting limits, and acting on your own behalf. In this chapter, you'll learn how to identify people who are emotionally mature enough to engage in a mutually satisfying relationship. I'll also discuss how you can adopt new attitudes about relationships so that you can interact in ways that will help put emotional loneliness firmly in your past.

Unfortunately, adult children of emotionally immature parents can be skeptical that a relationship could enrich their life. Instead, they tend to think that rewarding relationships are a pipe dream, too good to be true. And beneath this thought, they typically fear that other people won't be truly interested in who they are. These negative expectations perpetuate emotional loneliness, but you can change them once you're aware of them.

The Lure of Old Patterns

Remember what John Bowlby (1979) said: all humans share the primitive instinct that familiarity means safety. Therefore, if you grew up with emotionally immature parents, you may feel subconsciously drawn to the familiarity of egocentric and exploitative people. Quite a few of my female clients who ended up in abusive relationships distinctly remember that, in high school, "nice" boys didn't appeal to them. In fact, they typically found considerate males boring, which unfortunately meant that if the guy's behavior wasn't selfish or dominating enough, there was no attraction.

For these women, self-centered males probably stirred up uncertainty in a way they found exciting. But was this actual excitement, or was it a shiver of childhood anxiety in response to a self-involved person who wanted to use them? One tenet of schema therapy, developed by Jeffrey Young (Young and Klosko 1993), is that the people we find most charismatic are subconsciously triggering us to fall back into old, negative family patterns. Young warns that this kind of instant chemistry can be a danger sign, indicating that self-defeating roles from childhood are being reactivated beneath the surface.

This chapter will help you turn that dynamic around. The key is to use your newfound observational abilities to find emotionally rewarding people to connect with, instead of repeating old patterns that will lead to further emotional loneliness.

Recognizing Emotionally Mature People

The sections that follow offer some guidelines that will help you recognize more emotionally mature people. Then, instead of unconsciously enacting old, familiar patterns, you can consciously choose to connect with people who show the positive traits discussed below. Whether you're choosing someone to date, finding a new friend, or interviewing for a job, you can use the characteristics of emotional maturity in this chapter to identify people with long-term relationship potential, whether you start out face-to-face or online. Nobody's perfect, but good prospects should have enough of the following characteristics to make the relationship enriching rather than draining.

They're Realistic and Reliable

Being realistic and reliable may sound humdrum, but nothing can take the place of this basic soundness. Think of this first cluster of traits as the physical layout of a house; it won't matter what color you paint the walls if the structure is awkward to live in. Good relationships should feel like a well-designed house, so easy to live in that you don't notice the architecture or planning that went into it.

They Work with Reality Rather Than Fighting It

Although they'll work to change what they don't like, emotionally mature people acknowledge reality on its own terms. They see problems and try to fix them, instead of overreacting with a fixation on how things *should* be. If changes aren't possible, they find a way to make the best of what they've got.

They Can Feel and Think at the Same Time

The ability to think even when upset makes an emotionally mature person someone you can reason with. Because they can think and feel at the same time, it's easy to work things out with such people. They don't lose their ability to see another perspective just because they aren't getting what they want. They also don't lose track of emotional factors when addressing a problem.

Their Consistency Makes Them Reliable

Because emotionally mature people have an integrated sense of self, they usually won't surprise you with unexpected inconsistencies. You can count on them to be basically the same across different situations. They have a strong self, and their inner consistency makes them reliable custodians of your trust.

They Don't Take Everything Personally

Emotionally mature people are realistic enough to not be offended easily and can laugh at themselves and their foibles. They aren't perfectionistic and see themselves and others as fallible human beings, doing the best they can.

Taking things too personally can be a sign of either narcissism or low self-esteem. Both traits cause problems in relationships because they lead people to constantly seek reassurance from others. In addition, people who take things personally often feel that they're being evaluated, seeing slights and criticisms where they don't exist. This kind of defensiveness consumes relationship energy like a black hole.

In contrast, emotionally mature people understand that most of us can put our foot in our mouth at times. If you say you misspoke, they won't insist on a postmortem to uncover potential unconscious negativity toward them. They can see a social gaffe as a mistake, not a rejection. They're realistic enough to not feel unloved just because you made a mistake.

They're Respectful and Reciprocal

Emotionally mature people treat other people as individuals worthy of respect and fairness. All of the following traits reveal their cooperative orientation, which will come out in how they treat you. You'll have the feeling they're looking out for you, rather than being solely focused on their own best interests. You might think of these traits as being like the elements of a house's infrastructure, such as heating and plumbing, that are essential to making it habitable.

They Respect Your Boundaries

Emotionally mature people are innately courteous because they naturally honor boundaries. They're looking for connection and closeness, not intrusion. For emotionally immature people, on the other hand, getting close to someone often leads to taking the person for granted. They seem to think closeness means manners don't matter.

Emotionally mature people will respect your individuality. They never assume that if you love them, you'll want the same things they do. Instead, they take your feelings and boundaries into account in any interaction. This may sound like a lot of work, but it isn't; emotionally mature people automatically tune in to how others are feeling. Real empathy makes consideration of other people second nature.

An important gesture of courtesy and good boundaries in relationships is not to tell partners or friends what they should feel or think. Another is respecting that others have the final say on what their motivations are. In contrast, immature people who are looking for control or enmeshment may "psychoanalyze" you to their own advantage, telling you what you really meant or how you need to change your thinking. This is a sign that they disrespect your boundaries. Emotionally mature people may tell you how they feel about what you did, but they don't pretend to know you better than you know yourself.

If you were neglected by emotionally immature parents during childhood, you may find yourself willing to put up with unsolicited analysis and unwanted advice from others. This is common among people who are hungry for personal feedback that shows someone is thinking about them. But this kind of "advice" isn't nourishing attention; rather, it's motivated by a desire to be in control.

Tyrone's Story

Tyrone's girlfriend, Sylvie, frequently took charge in ways that made him uncomfortable, and lately it had been getting worse. For instance, when Tyrone wanted to slow down the relationship, Sylvie analyzed this as a sign of what she called his "fear of commitment." She told him that he wasn't allowing himself to see her as she was now and was instead viewing her through the lens of her past behavior.

As Tyrone became increasingly unhappy in the relationship, Sylvie urged him to act happier. She kept telling him to smile more, because she missed that in him. But Tyrone was missing something too: a partner considerate enough to accept his feelings and consider the possibility that her behavior might be part of the problem.

They Give Back

Fairness and reciprocity are at the heart of good relationships. Emotionally mature people don't like taking advantage of people, nor do they like the feeling of being used. They want to help and are generous with their time, but they also ask for attention and assistance when they need it. They're willing to give more than they get back for awhile, but they won't let an imbalance go on indefinitely.

If you grew up with emotionally immature parents, you may face your own challenges with reciprocity, having learned to give either too much or not enough. Your parents' self-preoccupied demands may have distorted your natural instincts about fairness. If you were an internalizer, you learned that in order to be loved or desirable, you need to give more than you get; otherwise you'll be of no value to others. If you were an externalizer, you may have the false belief that others don't really love you unless they prove it by always putting you first and repeatedly overextending themselves for you.

Dan's Story

Dan originally came to therapy after the breakup of his marriage to a self-absorbed woman who exploited his generous nature and didn't give much back. In therapy, he realized that he'd sacrificed too much, violating the principles of fairness just as his wife had in taking too much. As Dan began to practice better self-care by not being overly generous, he noticed that he was becoming more interested in women who had a greater capacity for reciprocity.

Still, this new way of relating felt unusual to him at first. For example, after paying for an expensive dinner with his new girlfriend, Dan was amazed when she said she wanted to treat him to an upcoming concert. "You gave me a great evening," she told him, "and I want to do something fun for you." Dan was amazed by her reciprocity and generosity, and he was also able to correctly identify it as a sign of her emotional maturity.

They Are Flexible and Compromise Well

Emotionally mature people are usually flexible and try to be fair and objective. An important trait to keep an eye on is how others respond if you have to change your plans. Can they distinguish between personal rejection and something unexpected coming up? Are they able to let you know they're disappointed without holding it against you? If you unavoidably have to let them down, emotionally mature people generally will give you the benefit of the doubt—especially if you're empathetic and suggest trade-offs or compromises to ease their disappointment.

Most emotionally mature people can accept that changes and disappointments are a part of life. They accept their feelings and look for alternative ways to find gratification when they're disappointed. They're collaborative and open to others' ideas.

When you forge a compromise with an emotionally mature person, you won't feel like you're giving anything up; instead, both of you will feel satisfied. Because collaborative, mature people don't have an agenda to win at all costs, you won't feel like you're being taken advantage of. Compromise doesn't mean mutual sacrifice; it means a mutual balancing of desires. In a good compromise, both people feel that they got enough of what they wanted. In contrast, emotionally immature people tend to pressure others into concessions that aren't in their best interest, often pushing a solution that doesn't feel fair.

People who are in unhappy relationships often say things like "Relationships are about compromise, right?" But I can tell by their facial expressions that they aren't talking about compromise; they're talking about feeling pressured into doing what the other person wants. Real compromise feels different—as though your needs were taken into account, even if you didn't get everything you wanted.

Believe it or not, compromise can be enjoyable, not painful, when you negotiate with emotionally mature people. They are so attentive and connected that it's a pleasure working things out with them. They care about how you feel and don't want to leave you feeling unsatisfied. Because they have empathy, they won't feel settled if you're unhappy with the outcome. They want you to feel good too! Being treated with such consideration can make compromise a rewarding experience.

They're Even-Tempered

The sooner temper shows up in a relationship, the worse the implications. Most people are on their best behavior early in a relationship, so be wary of people who display irritability early on. It can indicate both brittleness and a sense of entitlement, not to mention disrespect. People who have a short fuse and expect that life should go according to their wishes don't make for good company. If you find yourself reflexively stepping in to soothe someone's anger, watch out.

There are enormous variations in how people experience and express their anger. More mature people find a sustained state of anger unpleasant, so they quickly try to find a way to get past it. Less mature people, on the other hand, may feed their anger and act as though reality should adapt to them. With the latter, be aware that their sense of entitlement may one day place you in the crosshairs of their anger.

People who show anger by withdrawing love are particularly pernicious. The outcome of such behavior is that nothing gets solved and the other person just feels punished. In contrast, emotionally mature people will usually tell you what's wrong and ask you to do things differently. They don't sulk or pout for long periods of time or make you walk on eggshells. Ultimately, they're willing to take the initiative to bring conflict to a close, rather than giving you the silent treatment.

That said, people typically need some time to calm down before they can talk about what made them angry, regardless of their emotional maturity level. Forcing an issue when both parties are still angry isn't a good idea. Taking a time-out often works better, helping people avoid saying things in the heat of an argument that they might later regret. In addition, people sometimes need space to deal with their feelings on their own first.

They Are Willing to Be Influenced

Emotionally mature people have a secure sense of self. They don't feel threatened when other people see things differently, nor are they afraid of seeming weak if they don't know something. So when you have an insight to share with them, they listen and consider what you tell them. They may not agree, but thanks to their natural curiosity they'll try to understand your point of view. John Gottman, well-known for his research into relationships and marital stability, describes this trait as a willingness to be influenced by others, and counts it among his seven principles for a sustainable, happy relationship (1999).

Men are especially prone to rejecting a partner's input, since they're socialized to be self-assured and to resist undue influence. When this cultural training goes too far, it can get in the way of harmonious reciprocity in intimate relationships. However, there's no gender corner on this market; plenty of women also refuse to be influenced by anybody and can be just as rigid as any man. Whatever the gender, unwillingness to consider someone else's point of view indicates emotional immaturity and a rocky road ahead.

They're Truthful

Telling the truth is the basis of trust and a sign of a person's level of integrity. In addition, it shows respect for the other person's experience. Emotionally mature people understand why you're upset if they lie or give you a false impression.

Telling the absolute truth can be hard for all of us at times, for many reasons. For example, when we have to interact with an angry or critical person, we may be inclined to lie for self-protection. But you can count on an emotionally mature person to be genuine and forthcoming when honesty really counts.

They Apologize and Make Amends

Emotionally mature people want to be responsible for their own behavior and are willing to apologize when needed. This kind of basic respect and reciprocity mends injured trust and hurt feelings and helps maintain good relationships.

Although emotionally immature people may also offer apologies, these are often nothing more than lip service, designed to placate others without a real intent to change (Cloud and Townsend 1995). Such apologies have no heart in them and typically feel more like an evasion than relationship repair. People who are sincere, on the other hand, won't just apologize; they'll also make a clear statement about how they intend to do things differently.

When you tell people that they've hurt or disappointed you, observe their response. Do they just defend themselves, or do they try to change?

Do they apologize just to appease you, or do they understand and care about what you felt?

——————Crystal's Story——————

Crystal found e-mail evidence that her husband, Marcos, was having an affair. Marcos begged for forgiveness, but the fallout from her discovery almost ended their marriage. After a temporary separation, Crystal decided that she was willing to work on the relationship, but one of her conditions was that they keep talking about what had happened. She needed to understand, and she needed more details. Marcos couldn't fathom this and told her, "I said I'm sorry. What more do you want? Why do you keep bringing it up? What do you want me to do?"

The answer was simple. Crystal wanted Marcos to self-reflect, explain why he'd had the affair, and know how betrayed she felt. She also needed Marcos to hear her out instead of shutting her down. People who have been betrayed are often consumed with getting all the facts. It may be morbid curiosity, but getting their questions answered can help them process their pain. It wasn't enough to just apologize; Marcos needed to be available to answer Crystal's questions as she struggled to understand what happened.

They're Responsive

Once all the basic traits outlined above are in place, you'll also want to seek out people with qualities that give relationships a sense of warmth and fun. Think of the following traits as essential to a fully rewarding relationship experience, just as paint and furnishings are essential to make a house a home.

Their Empathy Makes You Feel Safe

Empathy is what makes people feel safe in relationships. Along with self-awareness, it's the soul of emotional intelligence (Goleman 1995), guiding people toward prosocial behavior and fairness in dealings with others. In contrast, nonempathic people overlook your feelings and don't seem to imagine your experience or be sensitive to it. It's important to be aware of this, because a person who isn't responsive to your feelings won't be emotionally safe when the two of you have any kind of disagreement.

Ellen's Story

Ellen's boyfriend was largely incapable of empathy. If she tried to tell him about her day, he listened just long enough to use her story as a springboard to start talking about what happened to him. Eventually, Ellen worked up the nerve to ask him if he could listen and show more empathy, but he thought she was saying he was a bad person. He shot back that she wasn't perfect either. He couldn't respond to her emotional need because he could only hear her request as a criticism against which he had to defend himself.

They Make You Feel Seen and Understood

What a gift it is to talk with someone who's interested in your inner experience! Instead of feeling strange for having certain feelings, you feel understood because the other person resonates with what you're talking about on an emotional level.

When emotionally mature people find you interesting, they show curiosity about you. They enjoy hearing your history and getting to know you. They also remember things you've told them and are likely to reference that information in future conversations. They like your individuality and are intrigued by the ways in which you're different from them. This reflects their desire to really get to know you, rather than looking for you to mirror them.

Emotionally mature people see you positively and keep a mental library of your best qualities. They often reference your strengths and sometimes seem to know you better than you know yourself. In the climate of such interest and acceptance, you'll feel that you can be completely yourself and may find yourself telling the other person things you hadn't planned to or sharing a personal experience that you usually keep to yourself. You'll also notice that the more you share with such people, the more they share with you. That's how true intimacy develops and flourishes. Once they trust you, they'll engage in clear, intimate communication and let you into their inner world. If you've been emotionally neglected in the past, this may be a new and exhilarating experience for you.

You'll also discover that when you feel distressed, emotionally mature people don't pull back. They aren't afraid of your emotions and don't tell you that you should be feeling some other way. They embrace your feelings and like learning about the things you want to tell them. And you *will* want to tell them things. It's wonderful and validating to find someone who really listens.

They Like to Comfort and Be Comforted

Emotionally mature, responsive people have an emotional engagement instinct that works smoothly. They like to connect, and they naturally give and receive comfort under stressful conditions. They are sympathetic and know how crucial friendly support can be.

They Reflect on Their Actions and Try to Change

Emotionally mature people are capable of taking a look at themselves and reflecting on their behavior. They may not use psychological terms, but they clearly understand how people affect each other emotionally. They take you seriously if you tell them about a behavior of theirs that makes you uncomfortable. They're willing to absorb this kind of feedback because they enjoy the increased emotional intimacy that such clear communication brings. This shows interest in and curiosity about other people's perceptions, along with a desire to learn about and improve themselves.

Willingness to take action as a result of self-reflection is also important. It isn't enough to just say the right things or apologize. If you're clear about what bothers you, they'll remain aware of the issue and demonstrate follow-through in their attempts to change.

———Jill's Story———

Jill tried for years to get her husband to look at how he ignored her, but each attempt to solicit his empathy resulted in a counterattack in which he maintained that Jill was impossible to please. Over time, his refusal to engage in self-reflection shut down Jill's efforts at intimate communication with him. It wasn't surprising that Jill ultimately left her husband for another man— someone who did care about what she thought and how she felt. Her new partner reconsidered his behavior when she brought it up and then made an effort to do things differently.

They Can Laugh and Be Playful

Humor is a delightful form of responsiveness, and also a highly adaptive coping mechanism (Vaillant 2000). Emotionally mature people have a good sense of humor and can use lightheartedness to relieve stress. Laughter is a form of egalitarian play between people and reflects an ability to relinquish control and follow someone else's lead.

Emotionally immature people often have difficulty engaging in humor in ways that strengthen bonds with others. Instead, they push humor on others, even when others aren't amused. They also tend to enjoy humor at someone else's expense, using it to boost their self-esteem. For example, they may enjoy humor that involves tricking people or making them look foolish or inept. This trait is a good indicator of how they will eventually treat you.

Humor with an edge, such as sarcasm, is best served as a spice, not the main course. In moderation it adds a bit of pleasurable tension, but in excess it reflects cynicism, which is hard to live with as a steady diet. Too much cynicism and sarcasm are signs of a closed-down person who fears connection and seeks emotional protection by focusing on the negative.

They're Enjoyable to Be Around

Being enjoyable to be around is a somewhat ineffable characteristic, but it's crucial for relationship satisfaction. Reviewing the traits above, you can see that emotionally mature people have an overall positive vibe that's pleasurable to be around. They aren't always happy, of course, but for the most part they seem able to generate their own good feelings and enjoy life. One woman who finally found her life partner after a series of unsatisfying relationships knew he was the one because she always enjoyed spending time in his presence, even if it was just a trip to the grocery store.

What to Look For in Meeting People Online

The characteristics described in this chapter are also applicable to online dating and social networking. In fact, online contacts offer a great opportunity to practice identifying emotional maturity as you read and consider what people are revealing about themselves in their profiles and electronic messages.

Although some people are better writers than others, all personal writing reveals something about how people think, what they value, and what they're most focused on, not to mention their sense of humor and sensitivity to other people's feelings. Plus, reading what people have written gives you time to notice how their messages make you feel. Initial phone calls also give you room to observe and note what the other person is saying while keeping your facial expressions and nonverbal reactions private.

In these venues, ask yourself how you feel about people's timing and pacing. Are they respectful of your boundaries and how fast or slow you want to go in getting to know each other? Do you feel pressured for instant intimacy, or do they take an uncomfortably long time to respond? Do you get the feeling they're pinning too many hopes on you before they even know you? Or are they being a little standoffish, so that you have to work to keep the communication going? Are they reciprocal? Do they reference what you said in your previous e-mail or immediately launch into their own topics? Do they keep a conversation going by asking questions to get to know you better or find out your thoughts on a certain topic? Do you find it easy to schedule things with them, or are the two of you frequently out of sync?

After reading a profile, e-mail, or message, take a moment to jot down your impressions. This kind of reflection will help you learn to focus your attention on your gut reaction, which will be easier because you won't have the social pressure of a face-to-face interaction. Describe how you feel inside after reading what the person wrote. Will you feel comfortable being yourself, or will you feel like you have to watch what you say and how you say it? Observing your reactions is a crucial skill for identifying emotionally mature people, and online communication can give you excellent practice in doing just that.

Exercise: Assessing Others' Emotional Maturity

I've summarized all of the above characteristics in the following checklist, which you can use to determine whether a person will be able to give you the kind of relationship you want. If you want to complete this assessment for several people, use the downloadable version of this exercise available at http://www.newharbinger.com/31700. (See the back of the book for instructions on how to access it.)

Realistic and Reliable

_____ They work with reality rather than fighting it.

_____ They can feel and think at the same time.

_____ Their consistency makes them reliable.

_____ They don't take everything personally.

Respectful and Reciprocal

_____ They respect your boundaries.

_____ They give back.

_____ They are flexible and compromise well.

_____ They're even-tempered

_____ They're willing to be influenced.

_____ They're truthful.

_____ They apologize and make amends.

Responsive

_____ Their empathy makes you feel safe.

_____ They make you feel seen and understood.

_____ They like to comfort and be comforted.

_____ They reflect on their actions and try to change.

_____ They can laugh and be playful.

_____ They're enjoyable to be around.

The more of these qualities a person has, the more likely it is that the two of you can forge a satisfying and genuine connection.

Developing New Relationship Habits

Now that you can identify emotionally mature people, there's one last piece of the relationship puzzle to address: your own behavior. In this final section, we'll take a brief look at some new approaches on your part that can make your relationships more genuine and reciprocal. You can work on these actions to help your relationships flourish. After all, improving your own ability to interact in an emotionally mature way is an important contribution toward having the relationships you want.

Exercise: Exploring New Ways of Being in Relationships

Let's create a profile of emotional maturity that you can work toward. The following lists present a picture of how an emotionally mature person might interact and behave in relationships. Read through the following lists of new behaviors, beliefs, and values and choose a few to practice. Just pick one or two at a time, and be gentle with yourself as you work on them. Some might be harder than others.

Being Willing to Ask for Help

- I'll ask for help whenever I need to.

- I'll remind myself that if I need something, most people will be glad to help if they can.

- I'll use clear, intimate communication to ask for what I want, explaining my feelings and the reasons for my request.

- I'll trust that most people will listen if I ask them to.

Being Myself, Whether People Accept Me or Not

- When I state my thoughts clearly and politely, without malice, I won't try to control how people take it.

- I won't give more energy than I really have.

- Instead of trying to please, I'll give other people a true indication of how I feel.

- I won't volunteer for something if I think I'll resent it later.

- If someone says something I find offensive, I'll offer an alternative viewpoint. I won't try to change the other person's mind; I just won't let the statement go unremarked upon.

Sustaining and Appreciating Emotional Connections

- I'll make a point of keeping in touch with special people I care about and returning their calls or electronic messages.

- I'll think of myself as a strong person who deserves to give and receive help from my community of friends.

- Even when people aren't saying the "right" thing, I'll tune in to whether they're trying to help me. If their effort makes me feel emotionally nurtured, I'll express my gratitude.

- When I'm irritated with someone, I'll think about what I want to say that could improve our relationship. I'll wait until I cool off and then ask if the other person is willing to listen to my feelings.

Having Reasonable Expectations for Myself

- I'll keep in mind that being perfect isn't always necessary. I'll get stuff done rather than obsess over getting things done perfectly.

- When I get tired, I'll rest or do something different. My level of physical energy will tell me when I've been doing too much. I won't wait for an accident or illness to make me stop.

- When I make a mistake, I'll chalk it up to being human. Even if I think I've anticipated everything, there will be outcomes I don't expect.

- I'll remember that everyone is responsible for their own feelings and for expressing their needs clearly. Beyond common courtesy, it isn't up to me to guess what others want.

Communicating Clearly and Actively Seeking the Outcomes I Want

- I won't expect people to know what I need unless I tell them. Caring about me doesn't mean they automatically know what I'm feeling.

- If people close to me upset me, I'll use my pain to identify my underlying need. Then I'll use clear, intimate communication to provide guidance on how they could give it to me.

- When my feelings are hurt, I'll try to understand my reaction first. Did something trigger feelings from my past, or did the person really treat me insensitively? If someone was insensitive, I'll ask him or her to hear me out.

- I'll be thoughtful to other people, and if they aren't thoughtful in return, I'll ask them to be more considerate and then let it go.

- I'll ask for something as many times as it takes to get a clear answer.

- When I get tired of interacting, I'll politely speak up, asking if we can continue our contact at another time. I'll explain kindly that I'm just out of gas at the moment.

Do you get a sense of how much more energy and lightness you'd feel if most of these statements were true for you? You'd be active and self-expressive in your relationships, treating yourself kindly and expecting to be heard by others. You'd be freeing yourself from emotional loneliness. Even if you didn't learn these values and ways of interacting as a child, you can develop them now. Having emotionally immature parents may have undermined your self-acceptance, self-expressiveness, and hopes for genuine intimacy, but there's nothing to hold you back now as an adult.

Summary

This chapter outlined common attributes of emotionally mature people so that you can recognize such people more easily. It also briefly summarized new ways of relating that can help you create more satisfying and supportive relationships with others. Now that you know what emotional maturity really looks like, you won't be tempted to settle for the next person who shows you some attention or offers you the bare minimum in a relationship. You'll be able to look for what you want, and be comfortable observing others until you find it. As you reflect on your emotional strengths and capacity for connection, you'll find that the keys to happier relationships have been within you all along.

Epilogue

U nderstanding your past and embarking on a new future can be a bittersweet process. Shining a light on what happened to you and how it affected your choices can stir up sadness about what you've lost or never had.

That's the way light is. It shines on everything, not just the things we want to see. When you decide to uncover the truth about yourself and your family relationships, you may be surprised by what's revealed, especially when you see how these patterns have been passed down through the generations. Sometimes you may wonder whether all this knowledge is for the best. It may even seem as though it would be better not to know.

Ultimately, it depends on what you value about life. Is seeking the truth and self-knowledge an important and meaningful pursuit for you?

You are the only person who can answer this question. But it's been my experience—and countless other people's—that greater awareness brings its own gifts, most of which involve a fuller, deeper connection with the world and oneself. Working through a difficult past makes things in the present more real and precious. And as you come to understand yourself and your family fully for the first time, you're likely to appreciate life like never before. When you resolve your confusion and frustration about the behavior of emotionally immature people, life feels lighter and easier. My hope is that this book has brought you not only some understanding of yourself and your loved ones, but also some relief and the freedom to live more on the basis of your genuine thoughts and feelings, rather than outdated family patterns.

When I see the faces of clients who are discovering their true feelings for the first time and can finally recognize other people's emotional immaturity, their expressions reflect a sense of wonderment and peace. It wouldn't be too much to call it enlightenment. Not one of them would willingly go back to not knowing. With each bit of truth they encounter within themselves, they experience a feeling of self-reclamation. Despite any regrets they may have, an unmistakable sensation of wholeness comes over them and they feel as if life is starting over from this new point.

And it is. People who engage in self-discovery and emotional development get to have a second life—one that was unimaginable as long as they remained caught in old family roles and wishful fantasies. You really do get to start over when you open to a new consciousness of who you are and what's been going on in your life. As one person said, "I now know exactly who I am. Others aren't going to change, but I can change."

There's no reason you can't have a happy life starting right now. I actually think it can feel more rewarding to give yourself a happy life now as an aware adult than to have always had it from the beginning. To be aware and present at the birth of your new self as an adult is pretty incredible stuff. How many people get to be awake and aware for the emergence of the person they were always meant to be? How many people get to have two lifetimes in one?

So tell me, is it worth the pain to get to live twice in one life? Are you glad you've chosen the path of awareness?

Yes?

Me too.

References

Ainsworth, M. 1967. *Infancy in Uganda: Infant Care and the Growth of Love*. Baltimore, MD: Johns Hopkins Press.

Ainsworth, M., S. Bell, and D. Stayton. 1971. "Individual Differences in Strange-Situation Behaviour of One-Year-Olds." In *The Origins of Human Social Relations*, edited by H. R. Schaffer. New York: Academic Press.

Ainsworth, M., S. Bell, and D. Stayton. 1974. "Infant-Mother Attachment and Social Development: 'Socialization' as a Product of Reciprocal Responsiveness to Signals." In *The Integration of a Child into a Social World*, edited by M. Richards. New York: Cambridge University Press.

Bowen, M. 1978. *Family Therapy in Clinical Practice*. New York: Rowman and Littlefield.

Bowlby, J. 1979. *The Making and Breaking of Affectional Bonds*. New York: Routledge.

Cloud, H., and J. Townsend. 1995. *Safe People: How to Find Relationships That Are Good for You and Avoid Those That Aren't*. Grand Rapids, MI: Zondervan Publishing.

Conradt, E., J. Measelle, and J. Ablow. 2013. "Poverty, Problem Behavior, and Promise: Differential Susceptibility Among Infants Reared in Poverty." *Psychological Science* 24(3): 235–242.

Dabrowski, K. 1972. *Psychoneurosis Is Not an Illness*. London: Gryf.

Dalai Lama and P. Ekman. 2008. *Emotional Awareness: Overcoming the Obstacles to Psychological Balance and Compassion*. New York: Henry Holt.

Erikson, E. 1963. *Childhood and Society*. New York: W. W. Norton.

Ezriel, H. 1952. "Notes on Psychoanalytic Group Therapy: II. Interpretation and Research." *Psychiatry* 15(2): 119–126.

Firestone, R., L. Firestone, and J. Catlett. 2002. *Conquer Your Critical Inner Voice*. Oakland, CA: New Harbinger.

Fonagy, P., and M. Target. 2008. "Attachment, Trauma, and Psychoanalysis: Where Psychoanalysis Meets Neuroscience." In *Mind to Mind: Infant Research, Neuroscience, and Psychoanalysis*, edited by E. Jurist, A. Slade, and S. Bergner. New York: Other Press.

Fosha, D. 2000. *The Transforming Power of Affect: A Model for Accelerated Change*. New York: Basic Books.

Fraad, H. 2008. "Toiling in the Field of Emotion." *Journal of Psychohistory*, 35(3): 270–286.

Gibson, L. 2000. *Who You Were Meant to Be: A Guide to Finding or Recovering Your Life's Purpose*. Far Hills, NJ: New Horizon Press.

Goleman, D. 1995. *Emotional Intelligence: Why It Can Matter More Than IQ*. New York: Bantam Books.

Gonzales, L. 2003. *Deep Survival: Who Lives, Who Dies, and Why*. New York: W. W. Norton.

Gottman, J. 1999. *The Seven Principles for Making Marriage Work*. New York: Three Rivers Press.

Grossmann, K. E., K. Grossmann, and A. Schwan. 1986. "Capturing the Wider View of Attachment: A Re-Analysis of Ainsworth's Strange Situation." In *Measuring Emotions in Infants and Children*, vol. 2, edited by C. Izard and P. Read. New York: Cambridge University Press.

Hatfield, E., R. L. Rapson, and Y. L. Le. 2009. "Emotional Contagion and Empathy." In *The Social Neuroscience of Empathy*, edited by J. Decety and W. Ickes. Boston: MIT Press.

Kohut, H. 1985. *Self-Psychology and the Humanities*. New York: W. W. Norton.

Libby, E. W. 2010. *The Favorite Child: How a Favorite Impacts Every Family Member for Life*. Amherst, NY: Prometheus Books.

Main, M., N. Kaplan, and J. Cassidy. 1985. "Security in Infancy, Childhood, and Adulthood: A Move to the Level of Representation." In *Growing Points of Attachment Theory and Research*, edited by I. Bretherton and

E. Waters. Monographs of the Society for Research in Child Development 50: 66–104.

McCullough, L., N. Kuhn, S. Andrews, A. Kaplan, J. Wolf, and C. Hurley. 2003. *Treating Affect Phobia: A Manual for Short-Term Dynamic Psychotherapy.* New York: Guilford.

McGilchrist, I. 2009. *The Master and His Emissary: The Divided Brain and the Making of the Western World.* New Haven, CT: Yale University Press.

Piaget, J. 1960. *The Psychology of Intelligence.* Totown, NJ: Littlefield, Adams.

Porges, S. 2011. *The Polyvagal Theory: Neurophysiological Foundations of Emotions, Attachment, Communication, and Self-Regulation.* New York: W. W. Norton.

Siebert, A. 1996. *The Survivor Personality.* New York: Penguin Putnam.

Siegel, D. 2009. "Emotion as Integration." In *The Healing Power of Emotion: Affective Neuroscience, Development, and Clinical Practice*, edited by D. Fosha, D. Siegel, and M. Solomon. New York: W. W. Norton.

Spock, B. 1978. *Baby and Child Care: Completely Updated and Revised for Today's Parents.* New York: Simon and Schuster. (Original work published 1946)

Tronick, E., L. B. Adamson, and T. B. Brazelton. 1975. "Infant Emotions in Normal and Perturbed Interactions." Paper presented at the biennial meeting of the Society for Research in Child Development, Denver, CO, April.

Vaillant, G. 2000. "Adaptive Mental Mechanisms: Their Role in a Positive Psychology." *American Psychologist* 55(1): 89–98.

White, M. 2007. *Maps of Narrative Practice.* New York: W. W. Norton.

Winnicott, D. 1971. *Playing and Reality.* London: Tavistock Publications.

Young, J., and J. Klosko. 1993. *Reinventing Your Life: How to Break Free from Negative Life Patterns.* New York: Dutton.

Lindsay C. Gibson, PsyD, is a clinical psychologist in private practice who specializes in individual psychotherapy with adult children of emotionally immature parents. She is author of *Who You Were Meant to Be* and writes a monthly column on well-being for *Tidewater Women* magazine. In the past she has served as an adjunct assistant professor of graduate psychology for the College of William and Mary, as well as for Old Dominion University. Gibson lives and practices in Virginia Beach, Virginia.

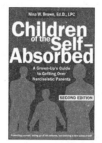

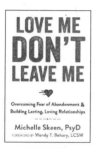

Register your **new harbinger** titles for additional benefits!

When you register your **new harbinger** title—purchased in any format, from any source—you get access to benefits like the following:

- Downloadable accessories like printable worksheets and extra content
- Instructional videos and audio files
- Information about updates, corrections, and new editions

Not every title has accessories, but we're adding new material all the time.

Access free accessories in 3 easy steps:

1. Sign in at NewHarbinger.com (or **register** to create an account).

2. Click on **register a book**. Search for your title and click the **register** button when it appears.

3. Click on the **book cover or title** to go to its details page. Click on **accessories** to view and access files.

That's all there is to it!

If you need help, visit:

NewHarbinger.com/accessories

new harbinger
CELEBRATING
40 YEARS